Author and life coach **Lorraine Turner** was born in England and later graduated from the University of London. She is the author of a number of published books and specialises in the fields of personal finance, business, property investment, life coaching, self-development and cookery. She has also built a substantial property portfolio using 'no-money-down' techniques.

Lorraine eventually swapped city life for a retreat on the English south coast, where she enjoys walking and jogging by the sea. She spends most of her working time investing in property and writing books, but also allocates a portion of her time to coaching clients, helping them to achieve their goals and create sparkling lives for themselves. In her spare time, apart from enjoying a busy social life with her partner, she has recently displayed a worrying interest in dressmaking, which she nevertheless hopes will be more successful than her disastrous attempts at pottery.

GET OUT
OF DEBT
FOREVER

Lorraine Turner

Vermilion
LONDON

First published in the United Kingdom in 2003 by Portal Publishing

This revised edition published in 2006 by Vermilion,
an imprint of Ebury Publishing
Random House UK Ltd.
Random House
20 Vauxhall Bridge Road
London SW1V 2SA

Random House Australia (Pty) Limited
20 Alfred Street, Milsons Point, Sydney,
New South Wales 2061, Australia

Random House New Zealand Limited
18 Poland Road, Glenfield,
Auckland 10, New Zealand

Random House (Pty) Limited
Isle of Houghton, Corner of Boundary Road & Carse O'Gowrie,
Houghton 2198, South Africa

Randon House Publishers India Private Limited
301 World Trade Tower, Hotel Intercontinental Grand Complex,
Barakhamba Lane, New Delhi 110 001, India

Random House UK Limited Reg. No. 954009
www.randomhouse.co.uk

Papers used by Vermilion are natural, recyclable products made from wood grown in sustainable forests.

A CIP catalogue record is available for this book from the British Library.

ISBN: 9780091910457 (from January 2007)
ISBN: 0091910455

Printed and bound in Great Britain by Mackays of Chatham plc

Copies are available at special rates for bulk orders.
Contact the sales development team on 020 7840 8487 or visit www.booksforpromotions.co.uk for more information.

This book is dedicated to Kitty

Note

The information in this book is general in nature and is not intended to constitute specific financial advice. The reader should therefore consult a qualified independent financial adviser before making any important financial decisions. While every care has been taken to present the information in this book as accurately as possible, neither the author nor the publisher can take responsibility for any errors, inaccuracies or omissions, howsoever caused. The references to websites, clubs, companies and other organisations in this book are given for information purposes only and are not a recommendation. The reader should always rely on his or her own research, and carefully check the credentials of all individuals and organisations before using their services.

CONTENTS

Acknowledgements ix

Foreword xi

Introduction xv

1 Facing up to it 1

2 Getting help 19

3 Increasing your income 39

4 Cutting your outgoings 55

5 Spy on your spending 73

6 Reward yourself 89

7 Time is money 115

8 Understanding borrowing and lending 133

9 Managing your money 155

10 Bargain hunting and shopping for free 171

Useful addresses 189

Glossary 207

Further reading 211

Index 213

ACKNOWLEDGEMENTS

The author would like to thank many organisations for their help with the research of this book, in particular Business Debtline; Citizens Advice Scotland; Consumer Credit Counselling Service; Ebay; Ebid; Financial Services Authority; Harden's Limited; National Association of Citizens Advice Bureaux; National Debtline; National Trust; Northern Ireland Association of Citizens Advice Bureaux; the Tourist Information Centres in Belfast, Birmingham, Cardiff, Glasgow, London, Manchester and Plymouth; and UK Insolvency Helpline.

Lorraine would also like to thank all the staff at Vermilion for their expert help, particularly Fiona MacIntyre, Clare Hulton, Julia Kellaway and publicist Ed Griffiths, and special thanks to Imogen Fortes, whose attention to editorial detail and understanding of the aims of this work have been greatly appreciated.

FOREWORD

Debt is a powerful tool, but it is also dangerous. This double edge is reflected even in the language we use to describe it. Call it debt and it sounds bad. Call it credit and it sounds good. Call it leverage and it sounds almost magical. In fact, all these words mean the same thing. Debt can be both useful and destructive but, like all powerful tools, it is important that those who use it not only understand the power it has but make sure they use it responsibly as well.

Although the UK has got richer in recent years, its citizens have got more in debt, and for some the debt has become uncontrollable. The effects of too much debt are so much more than financial: they can mean losing control of your affairs, and they can wreck your confidence and ruin your credit rating. All too often, people who find themselves in too much debt bury their head in the sand, hoping that the problem will go away. It doesn't. Hiding from debt usually makes it worse.

There is also evidence that debt is now being used not just to buy the occasional luxury, but as a way of life. A recent survey showed that nearly a quarter of people are going into debt just to pay their household bills. What's even more worrying is that many people do not even know how much interest they are paying on their debt.

Many borrowers spend far too little time researching the market. They might spend days or weeks looking for the cheapest television and then just accept the finance offer made by the shop. You should spend just as long looking for the best finance deal as you do looking for the television. In fact, looking for the best loan can save you much more than finding the lowest price.

The finance industry rarely rewards loyalty. This is even truer of the area of credit. The only way to stay ahead of the game is to move your business from one lender to another as rates change to make sure you always get the best deal. In fact, ever-larger proportions of building society business are not loans for new purchases but people remortgaging their homes looking for cheaper loans. That might not be good news for the lenders involved, but it does show that power is shifting from the lenders to ordinary people, which is good news for most of us.

A viewer once wrote to me complaining about the way I referred to so-called 'good' and 'bad' debt. His view was that debt was bad because you should save to spend. For him it was a moral issue. Somehow getting something you hadn't saved for was wrong, and in many ways I understand and agree. But this view is also a little too simplistic. For instance, a mortgage that helps you invest in an increasingly valuable property is a much more responsible and profitable way to borrow than a loan taken to pay for a new television.

In addition to borrowing for the right reason, it is vital to borrow from the right source. The most convenient way to borrow money is often the most expensive. It's easy to run up a big bill on your credit card, but it's also one of the more expensive ways to get a loan. Search around and you can find cheaper sources, which means you can afford to buy more.

Unfortunately, as the old joke goes, credit is offered only to those who don't need it. If you've got lots of money, people are more willing to lend to you. Those who actually need the money often find it harder to get loans and, when they do, are charged more for them. The world of debt or credit is not a fair one. What's important is that you know the rules and use them to your advantage. It's essential to read and learn about the world of credit long before you find yourself in trouble.

That's why I think a book like this is so useful. Now that debt has become so much a part of the financial landscape, it's important that those of us who use debt or credit make sure we understand how to get the most out of this financial tool without getting injured in the process.

Adam Shaw, co-presenter of BBC2's Working Lunch

Adam Shaw was the Plain English Campaign's Broadcaster of the Year and has worked on most of the leading financial programmes on television and radio. He is currently a presenter of BBC2's *Working Lunch* programme, which reports on business, finance and consumer affairs. He has written four books: a fun political quote book called *Political Rhubarb*, and three financial guides: *Money and How to Make More Of It, Managing Credit* and *Investing Basics*.

INTRODUCTION

The idea for this book came after I realised just how many people out there are struggling with debt. I can identify with them because I too have grappled with debt in the past. Without the right help and advice, it can be an overwhelming task.

One of the main difficulties of getting out of debt is having to deprive yourself of many of life's luxuries. For many of us, this is a significant stumbling block to paying off what we owe. It is fairly easy to be strict for a week or so, but following a serious long-term budget that doesn't leave room for a good social life, or whatever it is that we usually enjoy, is courting disaster and makes the whole process that much harder. I realised I would have to tackle that problem if my debt-clearing strategy was to have any chance of succeeding.

I researched and pored over this problem until I was able to devise a perfectly realistic, workable way of getting out of debt that didn't involve having to give up all of life's comforts. This book is the result of that work. It aims to help people get out of debt quickly and easily, without having to deprive themselves.

If you have been used to having regular holidays, an active social life, a varied wardrobe or whatever it is that you enjoy most, it will come as a relief to know that you don't have to give up these pleasures in order to pay off your debts. Just as a slimmer needs to follow a diet that allows for the odd treat or two, anyone wanting to clear their debts needs to adopt a plan that will allow them to enjoy life along the way. This book will show you how you can have your treats, and still experience the satisfaction of seeing your debts disappear. And for those of you who have rarely been able to afford treats in the past, this book will be a revelation. Many of you may find that your standard of living actually improves after putting these methods into practice.

The national figures for debt are depressing. Citizens Advice Bureaux all over the UK are reporting a sharp rise in the number of people coming to see them with large debts. Consumer debt problems associated with store cards, mail order, hire purchase repayments, loans, overdrafts and credit cards are increasing at an alarming rate, fuelling fears that people are being encouraged to borrow more than they can afford. In England and Wales alone, the Citizens Advice Bureaux are handling nearly one million general debt enquiries a year, of which over half a million are new consumer debt problems.

Although these figures are staggering, they are not surprising when we think about the variety of loans on offer nowadays. Loans for cars, home improvements, luxury holidays – in fact, loans for almost anything – have become much more widely available. It seems that almost anyone can borrow money these days. In many cases, you don't even need to prove your income. On top of this, offers of credit, debit and store cards come fluttering through our letterboxes daily. It's easy to see why so many people are in debt.

There are also many more products to tempt us than there used to be, as a walk into any shopping centre will demonstrate. Recent advances in technology, for example, have given us a wider choice of computer equipment and household gadgets, which are being 'improved' all the time to keep us buying the latest version, from the latest computerised organiser or mobile phone to the most up-to-date robotic vacuum cleaner. These ingenious, expensive and often unnecessary gadgets can take a will of iron to resist.

Clever advertising assails us wherever we go. Placards and posters, radio and television commercials, junk mail and magazine advertisements are everywhere, and wily branding and attractive packaging leave us desperate to own that irresistible something that all too often ends up finding its way to the rubbish pile or the local jumble sale.

Then there is fashion. How many times has the latest trend encouraged us to dump last season's perfectly usable clothes, hairstyle or furnishings in favour of this year's 'look'? Even food has trends nowadays – from French haute cuisine to Mongolian firepots – and requires the latest equipment, from Agas to wood-burning ovens.

Little wonder, then, that so much of this nation is in debt. The trouble with debt, apart from the stress and worry it causes, is that it costs so much money. Again, the Citizens Advice Bureaux have reported some distressing cases on their files. One 65-year-old man, for example, took out a £2,600 loan and will have to repay over £14,000 by the end of the 15-year loan period. So the price tag on whatever he used the money for was really a whopping £14,000 and not the £2,600 he originally anticipated. Another case involved a 37-year-old man who had a credit card debt of £600. He agreed £5 monthly repayments with the company, but interest was being charged at almost £6 per day. Three years later, that debt had grown to £4,500. Charges for missing a payment can be exorbitant too. One woman was charged a £15 fee for missing a monthly £4 repayment on her high-street store card.

Have you ever wondered why there is all this pressure on us to get into debt? The reason is, our debt is someone else's pay cheque. All that interest we pay each month is providing someone else with a regular hefty income.

That's why we owe it to ourselves to take control of our finances and get out of debt. The sheer peace of mind that comes from being able to write a cheque for something, and know you have the money in the bank to pay for it, is priceless. And it's surely worth the extra effort to know that the item you have just bought will cost you only £500, and not £1,500 by the time credit charges have been added. You could spend the money you have saved on something else if you want – perhaps a trip away in a luxurious hotel, a new television set or outfit – or save it for a rainy day.

This book will help you knock your finances into shape, however much or little you owe. I've used the techniques in it myself, so I know they work. You don't have to be good with numbers or mathematics or need any special skills to use them, just a sincere desire to get out of debt and a little patience. Even if you're lucky enough to have no money worries, you can still get big rewards out of this book: it will help you increase your wealth and put you firmly on the road to riches.

That road doesn't have to be dull either. This book will reveal how you can have fun while you're putting the sparkle back into your finances. No matter how serious your financial problems, you can enjoy an excellent lifestyle and standard of living while your bank balance recovers. This book will show you how. It will help you experience the freedom from worry that a debtless life can bring – and that's priceless.

Lorraine Turner

1 FACING UP TO IT

The first step on the road to financial freedom doesn't have to be hard, but you do need to be a little patient and honest with yourself. Before you can sort things out, you need to know where you are financially, exactly how much you owe, and how much money you have coming in. You also need to understand why you got into debt in the first place.

People get into debt for all sorts of reasons. Some people lose their job, for instance, and suddenly find that they can't meet all their household bills. Some have to take on other commitments, perhaps to help support someone else. Sometimes failed business ventures land people in debt, and sometimes it's just a case of people miscalculating what they owe and their ability to pay. Broken relationships also force some people into debt. Having to manage on only one income – especially if there is a new home to maintain, furniture to buy and a family to support – can easily push newly single people into the red.

Depressingly, the number of young people getting into debt is also increasing. Many of these are students, who have had to take out student loans in order to support themselves through college. However, there is also a worrying rise in the number of young workers who get into debt. These people, who fall into the 18–30 age range, get used to a good lifestyle while they're earning an income and living at home with their parents. When they move out and start having to pay their own household expenses, however, they find it difficult to scale down their standard of living, and quickly get into debt. The year 2000 saw an initiative to incorporate education on all forms of personal finance, including credit, into the national curriculum in schools, and it is hoped that this measure will help to reduce the number of young people getting into debt. However, major changes as a result of this initiative are not likely to take place overnight, and in the meantime many young people are continuing to get into financial difficulties.

These are just a few of the reasons why people get into debt. There are many others. Some people find it very difficult to curb their impulse buying or to resist 'bargains', while others simply do not know where the money goes. There's no point in blaming yourself if you have financial problems. It's not productive or necessary to punish yourself or try to apportion blame, but it is vital to recognise the problem and take responsibility for putting it right. It's not enough to ignore the problem and hope it will go away, or hope that someone else – perhaps a partner, friend or relative – will bail you out.

If you find it easier to ignore the bills and hope they'll go away, you need to realise that those bills are going to keep coming. They'll sit at the back of your mind, weighing heavier and heavier, and no amount of hiding them in dark cupboards or drawers will make them go away. If you continue to ignore them, sooner or later they'll turn into reminder letters, and then into summonses, and then into knocks at the door. Maybe you're already at that stage, and know too well the anxiety that an unexpected knock at the door can bring. Maybe you haven't ignored your responsibilities, but for one reason or another things have deteriorated to the point where you're so overwhelmed with debts that you feel the situation is hopeless. But the situation is never hopeless. No matter what your position is, and however you got there, this book will show you how to overcome your difficulties, whether you owe a few hundred pounds or many thousands.

So take a deep breath, and if you have any unopened bills and letters, gather them up in a pile in front of you and open them one by one. Don't spend time worrying about what they say; it isn't productive and will only make you feel worse. Just calmly take a piece of paper and a pen, and make a note of the date of the bill or letter, who it's from, and the amount you owe. If you have more than one bill from an organisation, check whether they are just one bill with lots of reminders, or separate bills. If there is only one bill, simply clip the reminders underneath the original bill and write clearly on the top: 'One bill plus reminders, £79 owed' (or whatever the amount stated on the bill). If, on the other hand, they are separate bills, add up the amounts, paperclip them together (you may want to file them separately later) and write on the top: 'Three separate bills, £125 owed in total'. Do this with each bill and letter in the pile, then put them all to one side. Then gather up any other bills and letters that you have opened but not dealt with or paid. Add them to your list, then put them on the pile with the other bills and letters.

Now collect together your other, regular bills so that you can make a chart. This chart is also known as a 'financial statement'; you will find it very useful for pinpointing exactly where you are financially. You will need to include all your expenses on the chart, so don't rush it. Make sure you allow enough time to go through them all carefully.

Overleaf is a sample of a person's financial chart. Joan is divorced, with one school-age daughter. She works as a secretary and rents a two-bedroom flat for her and her daughter. She doesn't drive, so she doesn't have to pay car costs. However, she does have to pay bus fares to work and school, and when she goes shopping at weekends. She has over £7,000 of debt, which is spread over a credit card, loan repayments and hire purchase payments for a television set. Some of the debt was incurred just after the divorce, because she needed to pay for new items of furniture when she moved out of the family house into a flat. However, the rest of it has built up since then. This chart shows her monthly finances, and you will see that her monthly income after tax is £1,350. Her debts cost her £171 a month.

As you can see, Joan's chart shows her monthly expenditure and

JOAN'S FINANCIAL STATEMENT

weekly • fortnightly • monthly (delete as necessary)

Outgoings	£	Income	£
Rent/mortgage	346.67	Salary	1,350.00
Mortgage protection/		Pension	
endowment policy	-	Benefits	
Pension	50.00		
Electricity	60.00	Other	
Gas	60.00		
Water	25.00		
Council tax	80.83		
Telephone	80.00		
TV licence	10.49		
Building maintenance/			
service charge	-		
Ground rent (if applicable)	-		
School/nursery (incl.			
meals and travel)	21.66		
Child minder	-		
Child maintenance	-		
Food	260.00		
Clothes	50.00		
Petrol/fares	108.33		
Car tax (if applicable)	-		
Car maintenance & MOT			
(if applicable)	-		
Home contents insurance	12.36		
Building insurance	-		
Life insurance	10.00		
Medical insurance	-		
Other insurance			
Credit cards	55.00		
Hire purchase (to buy a TV)	19.00		
Secured loans	-		
Unsecured loans	97.00		
OTHER EXPENSES:			
Swimming classes, evenings out,			
and babysitting	212.00		
TOTAL:	**£1,558.34**	**TOTAL:**	**£1,350.00**

income at a glance. It is clear that she hasn't got enough money coming in to cover all her outgoings, and her debts are building up because she has a monthly shortfall of £208.34. Most of this is being caused by the cost of repaying her debts each month. However, there are lots of ways she can improve the situation. For example, she can apply for all the benefits she's entitled to but not currently getting, such as Working Tax Credit and Child Tax Credit, and there is also scope for her to increase her income and reduce her expenditure without sacrificing any treats such as her nights out. But more about these later.

For now, let's concentrate on what needs to go into your own financial chart. All your outgoings, even things like your television licence and any credit card protection policies, should be included. You can base your chart on a weekly, fortnightly or monthly cycle, but whichever you choose, you must calculate all your bills and income that way. For example, if you choose weekly because you get paid weekly, but you pay your home insurance once a year, you must work out how much that insurance costs per week. If your insurance costs, say, £100 a year, you will need to divide that £100 by 52 (because there are 52 weeks in a year). This will give you the weekly cost as follows:

£100 ÷ 52 = £1.92 per week

Likewise, if you are working out your finances on a monthly basis, you would need to divide the £100 by 12 (because there are 12 calendar months in a year). The calculation would look like this:

£100 ÷ 12 = £8.33 per month

If you are checking my figures on a calculator while you read this, you will have noticed that £100 ÷ 52 is actually £1.923076923 per week, and that £100 ÷ 12 is actually £8.333333 per month! Whenever you come across awkward numbers like these, simply take all the numbers to the left of the decimal point, and the first two to the right of the decimal point, and ignore the others. So £1.923076923 per week will be shortened to £1.92, and £8.333333 per month will be shortened to £8.33. You'll also need to allow an amount to cover holidays, Christmas and birthday presents. For example, if you take a £600 holiday each year, you need to work out how much to allow per month or per week for this, then add it to the chart under 'Other expenses'. Do you subscribe to magazines or belong to a club? Are you studying on any courses? Do you give anyone birthday cards or presents? If you do, run through each month of the year, estimate how much you spend, then total it up over the year and work out how much that costs you weekly, fortnightly or monthly, depending on the timescale you have chosen. Do the same with Christmas, and any other regular celebrations. You may be surprised at how much you need to allow each month for these things.

Next add anything else you buy regularly, such as books or music.

LIST OF REGULAR CELEBRATIONS

Mum's birthday	£20.00
Dad's birthday	£20.00
Steve's birthday	£20.00
Chris's birthday	£20.00
Mavis's birthday	£20.00
Ernest's birthday	£20.00
Frances's birthday	£10.00
Debbie's birthday	£10.00
Christmas cards	£15.00
Christmas presents	£150.00
Total per year	**£305.00**
(divide by 12 = £25.42 per month)	

Finally, don't forget to add spending money. Try to be realistic here. It's no good giving yourself a hundred pounds a month if in reality you're spending closer to two or three hundred. Think about how you spend your free time, where you go and what you pay for. How much do you spend on a day trip or an evening out? Do you regularly pay for a round of drinks or get a cab home?

This might all seem a bit laborious and detailed, but it's vital if you want to take control of your money. You need to know exactly where your money goes in order to ascertain your real financial circumstances. Having said that, don't worry about getting things exactly to the penny at the moment: it's important to be as realistic as you can, but you'll have an opportunity to adjust your chart later.

Filling out your chart

Overleaf is a blank chart for you to copy and fill in. Once you've entered all your outgoings, add any amounts from bills or letters you may have just opened. Some of them may already be covered in your regular bills, but others, such as one-off purchases, may need to be added in. Simply add them to the list under 'Other expenses', remembering to adjust them to your chosen timescale of weekly, fortnightly or monthly.

If you run out of room, you can add more sheets as necessary. Use as many sheets as you need, and remember to include everything you would normally spend money on in an average year. Once you've listed all your outgoings, add them up and write the total in the space indicated.

FINANCIAL STATEMENT

weekly • fortnightly • monthly (delete as necessary)

Outgoings	£	Income	£
Rent/mortgage		Salary	
Mortgage protection/ endowment policy		Pension	
Pension		Benefits	
Electricity			
Gas		Other	
Water			
Council tax			
Telephone			
TV licence			
Building maintenance/ service charge			
Ground rent (if applicable)			
School/nursery (incl. meals and travel)			
Child minder			
Child maintenance			
Food			
Clothes			
Petrol/fares			
Car tax (if applicable)			
Car maintenance & MOT (if applicable)			
Home contents insurance			
Building insurance			
Life insurance			
Medical insurance			
Other insurance			
Credit cards			
Hire purchase			
Secured loans			
Unsecured loans			
Other expenses			
TOTAL: £		**TOTAL: £**	

Assessing your financial position

Now that you've worked out how much you spend, you're almost there. To complete the picture, make a list of all your guaranteed income – that is, all the money you know you're going to get. This could be your salary, pension, interest from any savings or investments, state benefits such as Jobseeker's Allowance, and any other money that you know you'll get over the coming year. Take off any tax and National Insurance contributions where applicable so that you're left with a net figure.

When going through your income in this way, leave out things like birthday presents or Christmas gifts: you may know that your granny always gives you £10 for your birthday and another £10 for Christmas, but you can't be certain you'll get them. Your granny's financial circumstances may change, so it's best to ignore any presents from other people and just consider them to be an extra treat if you do get them. Likewise, if you often get the opportunity to do overtime, but it's not absolutely guaranteed and sometimes lets you down, you shouldn't include it. Just concentrate on the certainties for now.

When you've listed all your sources of income, minus tax and other deductions, adjust them to weekly, fortnightly or monthly in order to fit the timescale you have chosen for your personal chart. Then total them up and add the final figure to your chart. You should now have two total figures on the chart, one for your expenditure and one for your income. Pinpointing your true financial position is

useful tip

If you share your finances with a partner, you will need to sit down together and do a joint chart showing his or her expenditure and income as well as your own. This is essential to give you a true picture of your financial situation.

now simple: all you need to do is subtract your outgoings from your income, and see what, if anything, is left.

Let's go back to Joan's chart for a moment, and subtract her monthly expenditure of £1,558.34 from her income of £1,350. We can see that she has a shortfall of £208.34 each month. If she takes no action and lets this shortfall build up, after a year this will have added an extra £2,500.08 to her existing £7,000 debt, and that's without taking interest into account.

Here are two more examples for you to consider:

Karen	£ per month	Tim	£ per month
Total income:	850.00	Total income:	1,160.00
Total outgoings:	825.00	Total outgoings:	1,175.00
	£25.00 surplus		**£15.00 shortfall**

As you can see from these figures, Karen has £850 coming in each month, and spends £825. Her monthly income therefore covers all her outgoings, and she has £25 a month left over to save or to spend on a treat, as she chooses. Having said that, £25 a month is still quite tight, and if any unexpected large bills came in, she would have difficulty paying them. Tim's situation is worse: although he earns more than Karen does, his £1,160 a month doesn't cover his outgoings of £1,175. He's £15 short each month. Although £15 a month doesn't sound like a lot, it will soon build up. Over just a year it will amount to a debt of £180. After two years it will be £360, and will continue to build up. If he takes out a loan to cover that debt, the interest will push it up still further, and by year five he could have a debt of as much as £1,500, all from an original shortfall of just £15 a month.

The result

Go back to your own chart. Now that you have subtracted your total outgoings from your income, and know what your real financial situation is, you are in the strongest possible position to be able to control your money. If you have found that you have a comfortable amount of money left over and can't understand why you still seem to struggle, don't worry, help is at hand. We'll be dealing with this later (see page 73). If you have found that your income doesn't cover your outgoings, but that your spending is over by only a small amount, remember that, as Tim's case showed, small shortfalls are still important and shouldn't be ignored because they rapidly grow into bigger debts. The good news is, you'll probably need to make only a few minor adjustments to cover the shortfall, and this will be dealt with in detail later (see pages 83–4).

If your outgoings are much, much more than your income, you need to take urgent action to stabilise your position. But don't panic. This book will show you how to sort everything out, no matter how bleak the position looks now. You've now done the hardest part, which is working out how you stand financially. For that, you can congratulate yourself.

Taking action

If the amounts you owe have become really unmanageable, and your chart has shown that you won't be able to pay them all back, the time has come for urgent action. Swift action now will avoid more complications later. What follows over the next few pages is a plan that will help you deal with the immediate crisis quickly and effectively. This plan will buy you some time so that we can get to work on sorting out your finances properly on a long-term basis. In later chapters you will learn how you can still enjoy your favourite luxuries while your finances recover, but the main task at the moment is to get over the immediate situation.

The first thing to do is to arrange your debts in order of urgency. The most urgent debts are as follows:

- Your rent or mortgage
- Secured loans (a secured loan is any borrowing where the lender can repossess an item of value from you if you do not pay back what you owe – you should be particularly careful about any loans secured against your home)
- Electricity, water and gas

You should prioritise these debts because, if you don't pay them, you could lose your home or have your electricity, water and/or gas cut off. Other urgent debts include the following:

- Income tax
- VAT
- National Insurance
- Council tax
- Court fines
- Television licence
- Child maintenance arrears

If you ignore these debts, the authorities have the power to prosecute you and in some cases even send you to prison, so they should be tackled before less urgent debts. And if you have any absolutely essential items that you're paying for on a hire purchase agreement, and to have them repossessed would cause you great hardship, you should include them in your list of urgent debts. Note, however, that by hardship I don't mean sadness at losing a favourite piece of jewellery or some other luxury item! By hardship I mean something that will cause you genuine physical or financial difficulty, such as losing an item you need for medical reasons or an important tool of your trade.

Once you have identified the urgent debts, you can then look at the secondary debts. These debts are still important and should not be ignored, but they should take their place after the urgent ones. Examples of secondary debts include the following:

- Credit cards
- Hire purchase agreements for unnecessary items (in other words, luxury items that will not cause you great hardship if they are repossessed)
- Loans for items that have already been repossessed
- Store cards
- Telephones (unless they are essential – for example, for a sick or housebound person)
- Unsecured loans (loans that have not been secured on your home or another essential item of value)

Dividing money between creditors

When you have identified which of your debts are urgent and which are secondary, work out a reasonable amount that you can realistically afford to pay towards clearing them. If you think you can manage £100 per month, for example, and you have five creditors (people or organisations to whom you owe money), divide the money between them. Give more money to your urgent debts, especially to those owed the most money, and divide the rest fairly between the others. Don't worry if the amount you can afford to pay each creditor looks

useful tip

Don't fall into the trap of paying whoever shouts loudest first. The essential things, such as your rent or mortgage, must always take priority, so look after these debts first.

small in comparison to what you owe. Your creditors will prefer you to pay a smaller amount regularly than promise larger amounts and keep letting them down.

Check the interest rate you are being charged for each debt. Wherever possible, prioritise the debt with the highest interest rate first. In other words, if you are paying 10 per cent interest on one debt and 15 per cent on another, then allocate a larger proportion of your money to the debt with the 15 per cent interest.

When you have worked out the amounts you can afford to pay, write to all your creditors. Make sure that you write to everyone, because if you make agreements with only some of them, the ones you've left out will still cause problems later. Write to all of them instead of telephoning, and keep copies of your letters. In this way you'll have written proof of your attempts to sort the matter out, and that proof will be helpful if things ever get to court. However, if you have an impending prosecution, or are about to have your electricity or gas cut off, time is of the essence, so in this case you should telephone first, get the person's name, and then follow it up with a letter.

In your letter to your creditors, explain your situation politely and tell them why you can't keep up the original level of repayments. Offer them reduced amounts (considerably reduced if necessary) and explain that as soon as your financial circumstances improve you will increase the repayments. Enclose a copy of your chart showing your expenditure and income. Your creditors will probably ask you for this anyway, and

✪

useful tip

It is easy to be panicked into offering more than you can afford to pay, so stick to your guns and agree only to pay off debts at a rate you can reasonably manage. If a creditor is uncooperative or won't accept your offer, you should seek professional advice (to get expert help, see Chapter 2).

✪

providing it in advance will get things moving more quickly. It will also demonstrate that you have calculated your figures accurately and are making a reasonable attempt to resolve the situation.

Overleaf is a sample letter, which you can retype and send to your creditors. Just fill in the details where indicated. If you are writing by hand, make sure it is legible, and use block capitals if necessary.

Creditors are often helpful when they are contacted in this way. They are used to dealing with people who have run into financial difficulties and will certainly not be surprised when you contact them. However, if you do come across an unhelpful attitude, try to get in touch with someone more senior, such as a supervisor or manager. In this case a polite phone call to the senior person may be appropriate, explaining the problems you are having. Get the name of the person and make a note of any agreement made. Then ask the person to let you have the agreement in writing. If you can't get to speak with that person on the telephone, or you

would prefer to write, send a letter instead. Your creditor may ask for more information, which you should provide as quickly as

SAMPLE LETTER TO A CREDITOR

[Your name]
[Your address]
[Date]

◀ *Fill in your name, address, and the date here.*

[Creditor's name and/or company name]
[Creditor's address]

◀ *Fill in the creditor's name and address here.*

Dear Sir/Madam

Re: **[insert brief description of loan here, including any account number or reference if applicable]**

◀ *Give a brief description of th loan, and add th account number or reference.*

I am writing to let you know that I am unable to keep up the current level of instalments because **[state reason here: e.g. I have lost my job/I have had to take on the additional financial responsibility of supporting a relative/my partner and I have separated, which has meant an increase in my outgoings and a reduction in income].**

◀ *Explain why you have got into financial difficulty*

I enclose a statement showing my current financial position and should be very grateful if you would agree to accept a reduced instalment of £ **[   ] per [month/fortnight/week]** until my financial circumstances improve. I will, of course, do everything possible to rectify this matter in the shortest possible time.

◀ *State here the amount you are offering to pay, and how often.*

Thank you for your assistance, and I look forward to hearing from you.

Yours faithfully

◀ *Sign your name here*

[Print your name]

possible. If you still have a problem after this, you will need to get professional help. This is dealt with in the next chapter.

Although it is important to list all your outgoings, be careful not to include non-essential expenses on a financial statement to your creditors, or they will not take you seriously. For example, one woman included the cost of a manicure every fortnight: her creditors refused her request to reduce her repayments on the grounds that she was placing more importance on her nails than on paying back their money!

One thing to watch for is any change in who 'owns' your debt. If a finance company to which you owe money is taken over by another organisation, this may work to your advantage because the new company may agree to better terms for repaying your debt. However, it can also bring problems. The Citizens Advice Bureau reported a case where a man had borrowed £7,000 and then become unemployed. He managed to keep making monthly repayments of £116, and the finance company in turn agreed to freeze the interest so that the debt didn't increase. However, the company was eventually taken over and the new owners decided to 'reapply all previously suspended interest'. As a result, the man's debt rose to nearly £39,000. If you encounter any problems like this, it is crucial to know where to find expert advice, and all this is dealt with in the next chapter.

2 GETTING HELP

Sometimes financial problems snowball to such an extent that they become overwhelming. If your finances have got to the stage where you feel unable to cope on your own, or if you can't reach an agreement with one or more of your creditors, the time has come to seek professional help. However, you need to be very careful about whom you approach for help.

Some organisations out there are happy to help you sort out your finances, liaise with your creditors for you, and even pay your bills on your behalf, but their help comes at a high price. Fees vary from company to company, but as a general guide they are usually not less than 15 per cent of the money they pay to your creditors on your behalf, with a minimum charge of £25 per month. This means that you will be out of pocket by at least £25 per month on top of what you pay out to your creditors – that's an extra £300 a year – when that money could be going towards paying off your debts.

Other companies may offer you a loan so that you can consolidate all of your debts into one loan and make a single monthly repayment. Psychologically this may seem easier, but charges and terms for new loans vary, and you may find yourself paying more overall than you would have done on your individual debts. Even if you will end up paying less, there is often the temptation to increase your borrowing to include a new car or some other luxury item. All this means your debts will take longer to pay off. If you like the idea of having only one payment to make a month, there are other, less expensive ways of doing it. And there is absolutely no need to pay a company to help you get out of debt either, especially when there are organisations out there who will do the whole thing for you for free.

Getting expert help for free

Although you need to be careful when seeking outside help, that doesn't mean the right help isn't out there. The main thing to remember is that, if you're in debt, you don't have to pay a penny for professional help. At such a crucial time, when every penny counts, the last thing you should be doing is spending large sums of money that won't go towards clearing what you owe.

The good news is that there are professional organisations out there who will give you their services for free. Some will give you advice over the telephone so that you can sort things out yourself; some will send you free brochures; and others will do everything for you, from working out your finances and liaising with your creditors to paying your bills on your behalf and even representing you in court – and they won't charge you a penny for their help. The only money you'll need to pay will be one monthly amount that you agree in advance, and all of it will be divided between your creditors each month. Your helpers won't take any money for themselves, and every penny you pay will go directly towards paying off your debts. There will be no hidden charges and no 'professional fees'.

caution
Be very cautious about taking out new loans to pay off your debts. This kind of borrowing could create further problems later, and should never be undertaken without professional advice.

If you are wondering how these organisations can afford to give you their help for free, the answer is simple: they are usually sponsored by large organisations, often lenders and other financial institutions, so they don't need to get their funding from you. Here is a list of some of the organisations that will give you their help for free, along with details of the services they offer, and what you can expect when you contact them.

THE CONSUMER CREDIT COUNSELLING SERVICE (CCCS) (FREEPHONE 0800 1381111)

The CCCS has fully trained counsellors who will help you, every step of the way if necessary, absolutely free of charge. It won't even cost you money to phone them because they provide a free telephone number. Make the call, and if they have an office near you they will usually make an appointment for you to see one of their counsellors, who will then help you decide on the best course of action. This appointment usually takes between one and a half to two hours. If you need a debt management plan, the counsellor will work one out with you, in which you will be able to agree a figure you can realistically afford to pay each month. There will be no pressure to make you agree to an unnaturally high figure. Your counsellor will want to make sure that any figure you agree to is comfortable, realistic and within your capability. He or she will then contact your creditors, work out an arrangement with them, and pay them monthly on your behalf until your debts are cleared. All you will need to do is send your counsellor one payment each month for the sum you agreed in your meeting, and this will be divided among your creditors. If the CCCS does not have an office near you, they will sort out the whole thing with you over the telephone.

The CCCS is a charity, and is funded by creditors through contributions and donations. Although these contributions are voluntary, most major creditors have agreed to pay the CCCS a

15 per cent fair-share contribution on all payments received. This 15 per cent won't be charged to your account, so you can be sure that all the money you pay to the CCCS is going directly to pay off what you owe.

Since the CCCS started in 1993, the number of people it has helped each year has grown and grown. In 1999, some 50,000 people called the CCCS, and by 2000 that figure had risen to 70,000 calls a year. Since then the number of calls has rocketed, and the CCCS is now handling 200,000 calls a year. Interestingly, it is not the boom in property investment and mortgages that has helped to fuel this rise. The CCCS is dealing primarily with unsecured debt, such as credit cards and personal loans, rather than mortgages.

If you would like to contact this organisation, it is listed in the Useful addresses section at the back of this book (see page 194).

NATIONAL DEBTLINE
(FREEPHONE 0808 808 4000)

This organisation runs a free national telephone helpline for people with debt problems in England, Wales and Scotland. It currently handles over 60,000 calls a year. It gives free expert advice over the telephone and will also send callers a self-help information pack called 'Dealing With Your Debts' free of charge. This pack will help you work out a personal budget, deal with priority debts, work out offers of payments to creditors, and deal with court procedures. National Debtline also produces a set of 31 factsheets on a range of topics including mortgage shortfalls; negative equity; how to deal with business debts; homelessness; reducing instalments on a County Court Judgement (CCJ); what to do about debts when someone dies; and personal bankruptcy. They send out these factsheets free of charge to people in debt, but agencies and professionals have to pay for them. This organisation is a member of the

Telephone Helplines Association, Advice UK and the Money Advice Association. It also has the Community Legal Services quality mark. It is funded by the Department of Trade and Industry (DTI) and major banks including Abbey National, HSBC, Barclays, Royal Bank of Scotland, NatWest, Lloyds TSB and Halifax, as well as American Express. They have also been part of the Money Advice Trust since 2002. If you would like to contact National Debtline, see Useful addresses, page 195.

CITIZENS ADVICE BUREAU (CAB)

You can get lots of help from your local Citizens Advice Bureau. The CAB service is the largest single provider of free, confidential and independent debt advice in the UK. It delivers advice from over 2,000 different outlets across England, Wales, Scotland and Northern Ireland. In Scotland, the CAB belongs to a separate organisation called Citizens Advice Scotland, and in Northern Ireland it is also separate and known as the Northern Ireland Association of Citizens Advice Bureaux. The CAB service is funded by grants from the Department of Trade and Industry (DTI), local authorities and private donations. Their help is free to everyone, regardless of age, race, gender, sexuality or disability.

All Citizens Advice Bureaux offer help with money problems. Many have a qualified money adviser available, and in some areas there are specialist CAB money advice units providing a full-time service. All CAB advisers can deal with emergencies – for example, if you're at risk of losing your home through repossession, having essential services such as electricity cut off, having belongings seized by bailiffs, or even being imprisoned. Whatever your money worries, CAB advisers can help you draw up a financial statement and check that you are not missing out on any benefits and tax allowances. They can help you sort out which debts are most urgent and negotiate realistic repayment terms with your creditors. In appropriate cases they will also help you get the interest frozen on what you owe, to stop your debts from mounting up. And if you have no money at all, they can negotiate an agreement that all action is withheld until your circumstances improve. In exceptional cases they may even arrange for your debt to be written off completely.

Most bureaux can also help prepare papers if you have to go to court, and may attend court to represent or support you. CAB debt specialists can also advise on bankruptcy and small business debts. Whatever your situation, your CAB adviser will be able to help, and will give expert advice in a way that helps you take control of managing your debt problems for yourself. You can find your nearest Citizens Advice Bureau in your local telephone directory or by calling directory enquiries. In addition, head office addresses, telephone numbers and websites are given at the back of this book (see Useful addresses, pages 194–5).

THE UK INSOLVENCY HELPLINE
(FREEPHONE 0800 074 6918)

This organisation operates a national telephone helpline for people with debt problems in England, Wales, Scotland and Northern Ireland. The service is confidential, independent and fully funded by the credit and insolvency industry. It is completely free to individuals (companies have to pay).

The UK Insolvency Helpline is committed to discussing debt problems and the options available to you. Their specialist advice is backed up with written self-help materials that can be sent out for free. If your circumstances meet certain criteria, they may also be able to arrange an Individual Voluntary Arrangement or Debt Management Plan for you for free.

This organisation is quickly establishing an impressive reputation as a debt management provider for both the advice sector and the credit industry. It enjoys widespread support and is overseen by an independent board of trustees comprising representatives from the money advice sector as well as the credit industry. It employs trained money advice professionals and can help with any level of debt from utility arrears to major insolvency problems.

The service works with clients from many organisations including trade unions and employers. It has close links with all of the money advice groups concerned in consumer rights issues and changes in social policy so that it consistently complies with the highest industry standards.

Among other benefits, the UK Insolvency Helpline:

O Offers immediate advice to all clients.

O Ensures clients understand the options open to them in order that debt repayment programmes are realistic and achievable.

O Offers advice without asking for sensitive personal information.

O Provides continued personal support and advice, assigning each client a case officer who is available throughout the repayment programme for help with concerns or problems that may arise.

O Gives clients a specific date by which they will have cleared their debts.

O Offers a nationwide network of support with home visits arranged in circumstances where this is felt necessary.

MONEY ADVICE CENTRES

These centres are scattered around the country. In addition to giving you advice, some of them will also take matters up on your behalf. One word of caution, however: there is a sharp distinction between voluntary sector advice centres, which offer their services for free, and certain fee-charging 'advice centres', some of which may even have names that sound like they are voluntary or public bodies. When in doubt, therefore, always ask if there is a charge for any of their services before accepting their advice or help. Many money advice centres are run by independent charities and won't make a charge, but it's always best to make sure by asking first. To find a money centre near you, look in your local telephone directory or contact directory enquiries. Your local Citizens Advice Bureau will also be able to tell you where your nearest money advice centre is located.

HELP FOR SMALL BUSINESSES

If your business has run into financial difficulties, then Business Debtline may be just the thing for you. It was launched in 1992 to provide advice to small businesses. At first it focused on the Birmingham area, but in 2000 it launched a telephone helpline to cover the whole of England and Wales, and from January 2005 it has also been able to advise callers from Scotland. In January 2004 the service became part of Money Advice Trust (MAT), a charity formed in 1991 and a leading organisation promoting free, independent money advice. The new service is funded by the DTI's Small Business Service and 12 major banks.

Through telephone advice and assisted self-help material, Business Debtline advisers can provide guidance on most debt problems a business may face. These include: how to prepare a business budget, prioritise all debts, deal with court proceedings, understand bankruptcy and limited company insolvency, avoid repossession of property, deal with tax matters, and negotiate with creditors and bailiffs. Callers receive a free information pack called 'Dealing with your Business Debts', which shows you how to tackle a multiple debt situation.

In a survey sent out to a sample of callers who received the information pack, 88 per cent of callers rated the advice 'useful' or 'very useful' and 98 per cent of callers said they would use the service again.

In 2005, Business Debtline handled approximately 8,000 calls. This figure is predicted to rise in line with the expansion of the service and recruitment of further advisers.

Business Debtline advisers can help business people from all walks of life to sort out their debts and increase their income by getting extra benefits and tax allowances. For example, you may be entitled to apply for the Working Tax Credit. This is administered by HM Revenue & Customs (HMRC), the new department responsible for the business of the former Inland Revenue and HM Customs and Excise. You will be able to claim the Working Tax Credit if you are working and on a low income. You may also be able

caution

Whenever you approach debt advisers, be sure to ask if they charge for any of their services. If they do, refuse politely and go elsewhere. When you are in debt, every penny counts. You shouldn't have to pay when there is so much free help out there.

to get the interest frozen on your debts, and if you owe the HMRC money it may be possible to come to an arrangement with them. Your Business Debtline adviser can help you with all of these and many other benefits, tax credits and money-saving strategies. Your adviser may also show you how to cut down your outgoings and increase your profitability. If you would like to contact Business Debtline, see Useful addresses, pages 193–4.

Your local Citizens Advice Bureau can also give you lots of free advice and help with your business debts, so give them a call.

Borrowing from friends and family

Getting a loan from a friend or relative can have certain advantages. There is less formality and red tape in the arrangement, and often you can get much more favourable payment terms. However, it can also be a double-edged sword. If the person who has lent you the money can't afford to lose it, or will suffer hardship if you make a late payment, it can mean the end of a good relationship. And, unlike loans from professional creditors, a debt to a friend or family member is likely to get personal.

As a result, it can be a lot more unpleasant dealing with debts of this nature, and you should always consider all the alternatives very carefully before taking this route to consolidate your debts. It would be better to stick to financial institutions and pay the additional interest if you can, instead of putting a personal relationship on such a fragile footing. Competition between banks and other lending organisations is fierce nowadays, and you should be able to shop around for the best deal. However, if you have already run into difficulties getting a loan from a bank or other financial institution, this may be because your proposition carries too much of a risk. If so, would it be wise or fair to let your friend or relative take on this added financial risk?

If you already have a debt to a friend or family member and are having problems paying it back, the one thing you must do is communicate with that person. Talk honestly and openly – never let that person feel ignored or left out. In this way you should be able to come to a realistic and amicable arrangement. If you also have other debts elsewhere, you should get professional advice – a good start would be to contact one of the organisations mentioned earlier in this chapter. When you give your list of debts to your adviser, you should include the debt to your friend/relative.

Tackling the prospect of repossession

If your debts have reached the stage where you are worried about having your home repossessed, it is important to remember that in many cases repossession could be avoided. If, for example, you have very little equity in your home ('equity' means surplus value after the mortgage has been paid off), it would not be worth a creditor's while to repossess it, and you may very well be allowed to keep it.

In order to judge how much equity you have in your home, you will need to find out how much your home is worth. Contact at least three estate agents and ask them to let you have a figure. They may need to see your home first. Alternatively, if they know the kind of properties in your road and your home is typical of all the others, they may let you have an approximate figure without having to visit you. Since these valuations are free, and estate agents normally give them because they think you might sell your home through them, letting them know that you probably won't be selling your home at the moment and that you just want an idea of its value may trigger some unwillingness on their

useful tip

To find the true market value of your home, don't go by estate agents' asking prices for similar properties. These are what the agent would like to achieve, but properties often sell for less. Instead, check what similar properties in your area have actually sold for recently (completed transactions, not sales that are still going through). You can do this for free by logging on to www.nethouseprices.com.

part so be prepared to shop around if necessary. You may well find that valuations vary between estate agents, so you should get several if you can, in order to find a realistic value. You should also be able to get an idea of your home's worth by looking at how much similar properties in your area are on the market for – try checking the local newspaper or talking with neighbours.

You can also ask a surveyor to value your home, but you will be charged for this, so it is best avoided if possible.

Once you have a reasonable idea of how much your home is worth, work out how much you owe on it. Your mortgage lender should have sent you regular statements showing what you owe. If not, ask for a statement. When it arrives and you know the amount you owe, subtract the figure from how much your home is worth to see how much is left over. This figure represents the equity in your home.

As an example, suppose you have ascertained that your home is worth £85,000, and that the amount you owe on your mortgage is £80,000. The equity, or surplus, is only £5,000, and a creditor may well decide not to repossess your home for such a small amount. Indeed, after legal and administration costs, and other charges, the £5,000 will probably be swallowed up anyway.

Taking another example, let's say you still owe £80,000 on your mortgage, but the value of your home has fallen to £75,000. In this case you have what is called 'negative equity'. Since you are £5,000 out of pocket on your home, again a creditor would be very unlikely to seek a repossession order.

If, however, your home is worth £80,000, and you owe only a small sum on it – for example £30,000 – you have a substantial amount of equity and a creditor would be very likely to want to repossess your home in order to release that equity and use it to pay off the debt. Each case is different, however, and other factors may come into play to influence your creditor's decision. When in doubt, always seek competent professional advice, especially if you feel there is a risk that your home might be repossessed.

You should also take into consideration whether your debt to your creditor is secured or unsecured. If you have taken out a secured loan, you will have signed a piece of paper agreeing to secure the loan against your home or other valuable asset. This means that, if you do not pay back what you owe, you have given the lender the right to repossess your home, or whatever valuable asset you offered up as security for that loan. A mortgage, for example, will undoubtedly have been secured against your home.

If you have taken out an unsecured loan, you will not have had to secure it against an asset. You should therefore check to see which of your debts are secured and which are not. Give this information to your adviser, who will be able to tell you how to proceed.

Voluntary arrangements and bankruptcy

In a small number of cases, bankruptcy starts to appear as the only option left, but there may be alternatives before things reach this stage. For example, if you live in England, Wales or Northern Ireland, you may be able to enter into an Individual Voluntary Arrangement (IVA). You would need to get creditors responsible for three-quarters of the total amount owed to agree to it. If they do, you will have to pay them only the surplus money you have each month, after your living expenses have been deducted. This surplus will be divided between them, and after five years all your debts will be cleared. If you can get it, this arrangement is better than bankruptcy because you still have a lot of control over your affairs. A court will appoint a supervisor to take charge of your case and see that creditors are dealt with fairly. If goods are sold, the supervisor will divide the proceeds between the creditors after court fees have been paid.

Even before going as far as an IVA, you may be able to ask the court to issue an Administration Order, where an administrator will take a monthly payment from you and distribute it to your creditors. This arrangement will save you from having any of your property seized, provided that you can keep up the monthly payments to the court.

In Scotland, once a debt exceeds a certain amount, either the creditor or debtor (or both) can petition for a Protected Trust Deed, where a trustee takes control of the matter and distributes your surplus money and any assets between your creditors. You only need to get creditors responsible for two-thirds of your overall debt to agree to this, and you will have to part with only your surplus cash, and any assets, for three years before your debts are cleared. However, you will have much less control over your affairs until the three years are up.

If you are considering any of these arrangements, you should definitely take professional advice. All the organisations mentioned earlier in this chapter will be able to help you, free of charge.

If, after all the options have been explored, the only path left is bankruptcy, don't panic! Being in debt is not a criminal offence, and later in this book you will learn how you can still have a good life both during and after bankruptcy (see Chapters 6 and 10). In the meantime, you need to get good professional advice, but here is a summary of what happens.

When bankruptcy proceedings start, a Receiver will be appointed to look after your affairs. Your Receiver will be very used to dealing with these matters in a professional way, so there is no need to expect an ogre! You will need to give the Receiver information about all your debts and income, so it would be a good idea to take the personal financial statement prepared in Chapter 1 with you. You will also need to provide documentation, such as invoices, utility bills, bank statements and wage slips, to back it up. You should include names, addresses and account numbers for all your creditors. The easiest way to do this would be to give the Receiver a statement or letter from each of them.

Once the Receiver has all the necessary information, and the bankruptcy order goes ahead, you will be declared bankrupt for a fixed term, which used to be for a period of two or three years, depending on the amount owed and other factors, but has recently been reduced to one year. During this time you will not be able to apply for loans or credit of any kind, and all your finances – especially income – must be declared to the Receiver. You will be allowed to keep a regular amount to cover your reasonable living expenses, and, as mentioned earlier, you may also be allowed to keep your home under certain circumstances. You may also be able to keep things you need to earn an income, such as important tools of your trade. Any other assets will be sold, and the money from these – along with any other cash – will be divided between your creditors. At the end of the bankruptcy term, all your debts will be cleared and you will be able to make a fresh start. Note, however, that there may be exceptions to this. For example, you will still have to repay any outstanding student loans. They remain the responsibility of the (former) student to repay within the terms of the loan arrangement.

As mentioned earlier, there is life both during and after bankruptcy! It's not the end of the world, and once a bankruptcy order has been made, and everything has been handed over to the Receiver, many

caution

It is important that you disclose everything to the Receiver, and hide nothing. If the Receiver suspects you have been dishonest in any way, he or she can apply to the court for a Bankruptcy Restriction Order (BRO), which may last between two to fifteen years and can make your financial affairs very restricted.

people experience a huge sense of relief, as if a weight has been lifted from their shoulders. You'll be able to relax, knowing that your financial affairs are being sorted out by a professional. Many people who have been through bankruptcy have gone on to become huge successes, so just put it down to experience in the knowledge that things can now only get better.

Your credit file

This file is kept by credit reference agencies, and all the financial information it holds about you is confidential. The agencies will release this information only to bona fide enquirers who have a genuine need for the information, such as potential lenders. An enquirer must also be registered with the Information Commissioner and the Office of Fair Trading.

The agencies get information about you from public records such as the electoral roll, Official Gazettes and the Register of County Court Judgements, as well as from trade bodies like the Council of Mortgage Lenders. They also get information about you from any lending companies or banks that have given you loans. You may be surprised at how much information your credit file contains: it will show all your current loans, some past loans within a certain period, how many credit cards you have, what your credit limits are, and if you have made any late payments. It will also record any credit searches by lending companies over the previous two years.

Whenever you apply for a loan, credit card or mortgage, the lending company will check your credit file with one of these agencies. If your credit file contains a bad mark against you – for example, an unpaid debt or late payments – you may well find that your application for credit is refused. Your credit file is therefore very important and can have a big effect on your life. If you decide to buy a home, for example, and need a mortgage, your credit file can make or break your purchase, depending on the information it contains.

If you have made an arrangement to pay reduced instalments to any of your creditors, a note will be made on your credit file, which may affect your ability to get credit until the situation is resolved. However, if you are having trouble paying off the debts you already have, the last thing you should be doing is trying to get more credit.

The good news is that, after six years, any adverse credit information – even bankruptcy – is deleted from your file. The other piece of good news is that, under the Consumer Credit Act 1974, you have a right to see all the information kept about you. If you write to the credit reference agencies, they must by law send a copy of your file to you.

If you would like to see a copy of your credit file – and I recommend that you do so – the three credit reference agencies to approach currently are Equifax, Experian and Callcredit plc.

However, agencies have been known to change, so for an up-to-date list, contact your local Citizens Advice Bureau. And remember, even the most efficiently run organisation can make mistakes, and errors have been known to appear in credit files. For example, your financial details may have been linked with someone unconnected with you but who shares the same surname. So even if you think you have no black marks against you, it is worth checking your credit file periodically, just to make sure.

Some organisations send your financial data to one agency only, or to two or three on an irregular basis. Each agency may therefore have different information about you on its files. The only way to be sure that you get all the information is to get a copy of your file from all the agencies.

OBTAINING YOUR CREDIT FILE

To obtain a copy of your credit file, simply write to each credit reference agency, or apply online. You will need to give the following information:

- Your full name, including any middle names (and your maiden name if your name has changed)
- Your date of birth
- Your current address in full (remember to include your postcode)
- Any previous addresses during the last six years

Each agency will charge a small fee: you can check the amount with the agency concerned. You will need to enclose a cheque or postal order for this amount, and the agency will then send a copy of your credit file to you. Contact details for Equifax, Experian and Callcredit plc are given in Useful addresses on page 193.

CHECKING YOUR CREDIT FILE

When you receive your credit file, check it thoroughly to make sure that there are no errors. You will probably find that you agree with everything that has been recorded about you. However, if you suspect that something in your file is incorrect, you should write to the agency, explain why the entry is wrong and ask for it to be removed from your file. By law the agency will then have to reply to you within 28 days, either confirming that the entry has been deleted or explaining why it has to stay on your file.

The financial information relating to previous occupants of your address will not be shown on your credit file, and will not affect your own creditworthiness. However, the financial information of anyone with whom you have a financial connection, such as a joint bank account or joint mortgage, could affect your own credit record. The name will appear on your credit file, but you will not be able to see any of that person's financial information. However, potential lenders will be able to get access to it.

If you can show that you are not financially connected to someone, whether they live in your household or not, you can apply for a Notice of Disassociation. To use this service, you should write to the credit reference agency involved, giving the full names and addresses of the people involved, and the nature of the relationship you have with the person from whom you want to be financially disassociated.

Contrary to what is sometimes rumoured, credit reference agencies do not operate a 'blacklist'. As information providers, they are neutral and not on anyone's side. However, they do have an obligation to give accurate information and to comply with the law. So if you find that you reach a stalemate with one or more of these agencies, and you are dissatisfied with the way the matter has been handled, you can contact the Information Commissioner (see Useful addresses, page 192 for details) and ask for assistance. You should give:

- Your full name, address and telephone number
- Name and address of the credit reference agency, and the agency's reference number
- Details of the entry in question, why you think it is incorrect, and why you think it could be detrimental to your interests

The Information Commissioner may contact the agency first to ask for its view, and you will then be sent any comments the agency has made.

You also have the right to attach a 200-word statement to your credit file, free of charge, explaining the nature of your disagreement. Your statement will become part of your credit file, and will be included each time your credit file is accessed.

Everyone deserves a break

I hope that the information in this chapter will help to reassure you that there's lots of help to be had out there, and that even the prospect of bankruptcy is not as terrifying as it might seem. No one should ever have to feel unsupported or unable to get help. Free, friendly, expert assistance is available all over the country, whatever your situation and however much you owe. But once you have found an expert to help you and have made an arrangement to pay everything off, don't fall into the trap of thinking that it's all over and that you no longer have to think about your finances. You need to establish sound financial habits for the future so that your debt problems won't come back. The following chapters will show you how to do this. They will also show you how you can still have many of life's luxuries and improve your standard of living, even while paying off your debts. First, however, we need to lay a few more foundations to ensure your financial well-being over a longer period of time.

3 INCREASING YOUR INCOME

Now that you know your true financial situation, you will find it easier to calculate exactly how much income you need to cover all your outgoings. If you have discovered a shortfall, you will need to find ways of covering it as soon as possible so that your debt doesn't increase. If you don't have a shortfall, but you are spending all your income and money is tight, you need to take steps to improve your position in order to make life more comfortable.

Ideally you should aim to have enough coming in to cover your outgoings and spending money, with a comfortable amount left over to cover emergencies or unexpected bills. You should also be able to earmark a certain proportion of your income for savings each month. However, if any kind of surplus is difficult for you at the moment, that can come later. The main thing you need to do quickly is cover any current shortfall. We can deal with strengthening your financial position later.

There are many methods you can use to increase the amount of money you have coming in, both on a regular basis and through one-off sums, and we will be taking a look at some of them in this chapter. However, there are many others, so after you have gone through the ideas given here, take some time to explore other ways you can get more money coming in. Be creative: try to spot the money-making opportunities that are all around you in daily life.

State benefits

If you are unemployed, or on a low wage, you may be able to get help from the government. For example, you may be able to get Jobseeker's Allowance or Income Support. In addition to a weekly allowance for household and living expenses, you might also be able to get help with your rent or mortgage, although you should note that help with mortgage payments in particular has been scaled down by the government in recent years.

GETTING HELP WITH MORTGAGE PAYMENTS

The main thing to bear in mind is that you will be able to get help only towards the interest part of your mortgage – you will have to find the capital repayment part yourself. In order to qualify, you need to have a mortgage on your home, and you also need to qualify for Income Support, Pension Credit or income-based Jobseeker's Allowance. For more information, contact your local job centre or social security office, which you can find in your local telephone directory.

GETTING HELP WITH OTHER COSTS

You may also be able to get help with other costs or claim other allowances. Here are some of them:

- Housing benefit
- Council tax benefit
- Hot water and heating costs
- State retirement pension
- Pension Credit
- Child Benefit

- Statutory maternity pay or statutory adoption pay
- Statutory paternity pay (same-sex partners also eligible)
- Guardian's allowance
- Child support maintenance
- Widowed parent's allowance
- Home Responsibilities Protection (to help protect your basic retirement pension if you are unable to pay National Insurance contributions)
- Carer's allowance
- Disability living allowance
- Attendance allowance
- Statutory sick pay
- Incapacity benefit
- School meals
- NHS prescriptions
- NHS dental treatment
- Sight tests, glasses and contact lenses
- Travel to hospital for NHS treatment

This list is not comprehensive, but it should give you an idea of some of the many benefits available. You may be entitled to others, so check with your local social security office or job centre. For example, you may be able to get a community care grant, which you do not have to pay back. Alternatively, a loan from the Social Fund may be available, but you do have to pay this back; since your aim is to reduce the amount of money you owe, it would be better to find alternative ways of bringing in extra money.

State benefits change from time to time: some may be amended or withdrawn and others introduced. The many benefits available, and the conditions for entitlement, can be bewildering at first, so if you are unsure about what you can claim, or if you think you have been refused a benefit unfairly, contact your local Citizens Advice Bureau. They may be able to suggest other benefits and allowances too.

Tax allowances

You may be able to claim tax allowances, such as Working Tax Credit. This is designed to help people on low incomes, whether they are employed or self-employed. It can also include support for qualifying childcare, and you may be able to claim back up to 70 per cent of your childcare costs. Extra help is available for people working 30 or more hours per week, disabled people and people over 50 who recently returned to work after a period on benefit.

If you have children, you may also be able to get Child Tax Credit. At the time of writing, all families with children can claim Child Tax Credit if their income is no more than £58,000 a year (or up to £66,000 a year if you have a child under one year old). You don't have to be the child's parent to be eligible, but you must be the main person responsible for that child. You can get further information and an application pack from your local social security office, job centre or HM Revenue & Customs (HMRC) enquiry centre. You can also log on to the HMRC website at www.hmrc.gov.uk. There is a lot of useful information on state benefits and tax credits on the website www.direct.gov.uk/MoneyTaxAndBenefits.

If you have been working and paying tax, and you then become unable to work for a length of time, you may be able to claim a tax rebate for part of the tax you have already paid. If you are currently working, check that your tax code is correct. You may be paying too much tax. Simply correcting your tax code may help you get more money in your wage packet. In the first instance, ask your employer to check your tax code for you. Then approach your local HMRC office. HMRC also publishes helpful leaflets on a wide range of tax matters, and it is worth looking at these to see if you can claim any other allowances.

If you are working from home, you can claim tax relief towards the cost of running your business, from stationery costs and tele-phone bills, to travel, advertising and equipment costs (such as a computer), so check with HMRC to make sure you are getting all your tax allowances. If you are self-employed and do not have an accountant, it would be worthwhile consulting one to make sure you are paying the right amount of tax and are not losing out on any tax allowances. Many accountants will offer a free initial consultation, so remember to ask for one before you go along, and make sure that the person you choose is a qualified chartered accountant. To find one near you, contact the Institute of Chartered Accountants (see Useful addresses, pages 189–190), who will be able to give you a list.

When you meet the accountant, be sure to check his or her hourly rate for any future work, such as preparing an annual return to HMRC. You may well find that the time and tax savings involved more than justify the accountant's fee. If there is anything you don't understand in your meeting, don't hesitate to ask for an explanation. You should feel comfortable with your accountant and able to seek clarification on any information that is presented to you. If you are not satisfied, shop around until you find an accountant to suit you.

Insurance

✪

Have you got any insurance policies that could help your position? For example, if you have lost your job, do you have a redundancy protection policy? Are you entitled to a redundancy payment? Approach your former employer, and check your position with your local Citizens Advice Bureau if you are in any doubt.

Do you have a payment protection policy to cover a loan or credit card? A policy may have been set up when you first took out the loan or credit card, and you may be able to make a claim on it and get help with your repayments. The same applies to mail-order catalogues. Look up the original paperwork and contact the company concerned.

If you have suffered financial loss as a result of bereavement, are there any insurance policies you may have forgotten? For example, did the deceased person have a job? If so, his or her former employer may have taken out a death-in-service insurance policy, which could amount to a lump sum payment to the next of kin in the region of two to four times that person's annual salary. Check with the former employer – if the firm is large, try the personnel department first.

Increase your earnings

If you are already working, but have some spare time, could you do some overtime? If no overtime is available, how about getting a second job? Even a few extra hours a week can help to pay off your debts, and it doesn't have to be the most fascinating job in the world if it's only a second job to help you get your finances straight. Check the local newspapers and recruitment agencies to see what's on offer.

If you can't find anything suitable, how about working from home? If you've got a skill, such as typing, you could offer your services to local businesses or professional people working from home. If not, you could still offer something that many people need, such as a dog-walking service, house-sitting, DIY, window cleaning or cleaning/ironing. These services cost very little to set up – in some cases all you need is a telephone – but you will need to consult an accountant to make sure that you keep your tax affairs and National Insurance contributions in order. To find customers, ask your relatives, friends and neighbours to pass the word around. You could also put a card in a newsagent's window, or take out a small advertisement in your local newspaper. If you live in a neighbourhood where jobs and money are scarce, it may be worth venturing further afield into more prosperous areas in order to find customers.

Other sources of income

If you have grown-up children or other adults or relatives living in your home, make sure they are paying their fair share towards the household expenses. If you are looking after an elderly person, you may be entitled to a carer's allowance. Again, ask your local social security office for details.

If you have a spare room, why not consider letting it out? Any money you get from letting it, up to a certain value (currently £4,250 per year), is tax-free – that's around £81.73 per week. You may need to get permission from your landlord or mortgage provider first. You should also contact your local authority to make sure that you will be complying with current regulations – you can find the nearest office in your local telephone directory. Let your home insurer know as well.

You can choose for how long you want to let out the room – for example, six months or one year at a time – and if you decide not to renew the agreement at the end of the tenancy, that is your right. However, it is essential to get the right tenancy agreement drawn up, outlining the terms of the agreement, who will pay for what, and other responsibilities. This will save a lot of problems in case there is a dispute later. Printed tenancy agreements are on sale in stationery shops, but do not use them unless you are very familiar with your rights and the law. They can also turn out to be old stock and out of date, or you may end up using the wrong one, which could cost you dearly later. The best way to get the right tenancy agreement is to contact a solicitor who specialises in landlord and tenant law. It need not be expensive: as a rough guide, a tenancy agreement should cost around £75, but fees vary so shop around to get the best price. For details of qualified solicitors in your area, contact the Law Society (see Useful addresses, pages 190–1).

Turn your possessions into cash

One of the most overlooked sources of ready cash is what we already have in our homes. How many of you have a cupboard cluttered with old clothes, or a stack of books gathering dust on a shelf? How about that box of old music that hasn't seen the light of day for years?

If your mind is travelling to an old junk drawer or a cluttered attic as you read this, you will be looking at a potential source of quick and easy money. Unless you live the most minimalist of lifestyles, you are bound to have some clutter that you can turn into cash. And you'll be amazed at how therapeutic a good clearout can be. Try it with a drawer or a cupboard. It feels liberating to get rid of a pile of clutter and have a clear, orderly space. You will also have the satisfaction of turning your old junk into money when you sell it.

Whether or not you believe in the magical effects of clearing clutter, however, there is no doubt from a practical point of view that a life full of clutter leads to disorder, confusion, and, eventually, inefficient work performance or wasted leisure time. A cluttered desk, for example, will cause papers to go astray when they are needed. No one can work efficiently at a desk cluttered with unfiled papers and unnecessary objects.

If clutter can wreak that kind of havoc, what's the point of hanging on to it? It is much better to clear it all out and turn it into money. So start now. Clear a room at a time, or, if you have a lot of clutter, start with a cupboard or even a drawer at a time. Remember, if it's not being used, get rid of it.

IDENTIFYING CLUTTER

It's easy to go around your home and identify obvious piles of clutter, such as old clothes and books, but clutter can often be found in all kinds of less obvious places. What about old photos, for example, which often get stuck into albums and forgotten, or, worse still, hidden away in dark corners and cupboards? Cosmetics are another source of clutter: do you have a make-up bag or toiletry bag full of items you never use? Or how many aftershaves and shampoos do you have going to waste?

Unwanted presents are another source of forgotten clutter. How many unwanted presents are you storing that you haven't been able to bring yourself to throw away? What about that hideous item of furniture a relative gave you years ago, which you've never liked but always felt too guilty to get rid of? Unwanted presents often pose this kind of problem. You never know when your aunt might ask you about that particularly ugly ornament she gave you last summer, so you keep it in the garden shed, just in case.

The problem with this is that other people are choosing what you should have in your home. We all have different tastes, and it

✪

useful tip

When you start clearing clutter, have three large boxes ready. Label them 'KEEP', 'SELL' and '24 HOURS'. The '24 HOURS' box is for items you're not sure about: give yourself 24 hours to think it over, but be strict with yourself and decide within that time.

✪

is very likely that what one person likes another will detest. But it is your home, after all, and you should be the one to decide what goes into it. So keep only those items you really love, and get rid of the rest.

This brings us to one of the main difficulties of clearing clutter – the emotional aspect. Is there an item that fills you with remorse as soon as you think of getting rid of it? Family 'heirlooms' are often the culprits here. You may hate the vase you inherited from your uncle, but you can't face getting rid of it, so it sits in a cupboard out of sight, forgotten for years until the next clearout, when it will probably be looked at, dusted, and put back in the same cupboard. This is the kind of thing you need to tackle. If you don't love and use the vase, sell it: your uncle would probably be much happier knowing that his gift was able to help you financially when you most needed it.

If you're in any doubt about what you truly feel about an object, a good way to decide is to pick it up, look at it, and pay attention to the feelings it raises within you. If it invokes happy memories, or it makes you feel joy or pride at owning such a lovely object, then it should stay. However, if it provokes tinges of sadness, guilt, or frustration because you don't really want it, then it should go.

One of the most common excuses for not getting rid of something is 'It might come in handy one day'. Such items rarely do come in handy one day, and you have a far greater need now, which is money. By hoarding things for a later time, you are also putting the suggestion into your mind that there may be more lean times ahead, and this is counter-productive: it should be your aim at all times to think positive, and expect good fortune to come to you. Such a positive attitude can only improve your chances of succeeding. So make that item 'come in handy' now by selling it. If a day eventually comes when you do need that particular item, you can always go out and buy another one.

If, after all this, you still find yourself keeping too many things, you will need to be strict with yourself. This is a good time to do what I call my 'island shack test'. Take a few minutes to do the following exercise.

Island shack test

The purpose of this exercise is to help you identify how few things you really need in life, and how many things you can do without. The results may surprise you. Whenever you feel clutter creeping into your life (which it always does, eventually), and you have difficulty clearing it, do this exercise. It will help keep your life free from a continual tide of junk. Make clutter-clearing a regular part of your life. Aim to do it at least once a year so that you can weed out any unwanted presents and other things you have outgrown or never used.

1. Imagine yourself as the only person on a desert island. Your living accommodation for the next six months will be a little shack near a pebbled beach. The shack is wired for electricity: there is one light and one power socket. It has a very basic bath tub, a sink, a cooker, a bed and bedding, a chair, and a couple of hooks in one of the walls. In the shack's only cupboard there are plenty of matches, a bucket, and a fishing rod and tackle. The shack has absolutely nothing else. There are no soft furnishings apart from the bedding, no towels and no household cleaning items. There are plenty of fruits, vegetables and other foods on the island, and seafood nearby, so you won't go hungry. A freshwater stream is close by, so you have enough water.

2. You are allowed to take only two sets of clothes with you – one set for hot summer weather, and one set for the chill of winter. You can also take 12 other items. Those 12 items have to provide everything you will need in life for at least six months. What will you choose?

3. Write down your two sets of clothes and the 12 extra items. Your

12 extra items can be almost anything, but you can't cheat and say a wardrobe full of clothes is one item! Each item must be counted separately, but you could take a hi-fi system, for instance, and count it as one item. A CD would be one item. A book counts as one item, and each cosmetic – whether a bar of soap or a deodorant – counts as one item. A pair of socks counts as one item. You'll be on your own on the island for six months, so if you want a phone so that you can keep in touch with people, you can have one and this counts as one item, but you can't use it to get off the island or to order goods to be delivered! You can't have a computer or any item of transport.

4. Once you have chosen your 12 items, mentally put them in the shack and imagine yourself living that life. Use the items in your mind: imagine getting up in the morning, getting washed and dressed and eating your meals. How would you spend your time? Imagine yourself getting into bed at night, and living from day to day with the few items you have.

5. Repeat this process in your mind a few times until it becomes familiar, then bring your mind away from the island and back to everyday consciousness. Now walk around your home, taking the list of items from the island with you. Pick up the things in your home that match the items on the list, and set them aside. Then look at the remaining items that you have 'left behind' in your home. It should be easier to recognise where the clutter is now.

HOW TO SELL YOUR UNWANTED ITEMS

When you have gathered up all the items you no longer need, don't leave them in a box to gather dust. You need to sell them as quickly as possible. If you have a lot of items to sell, you may need to do it in stages, but keep at it.

There are many ways you can sell your unwanted items: your customers may be friends, relatives and neighbours, for instance, or you could do a garage sale. You could also put a small advertisement in your local newspaper. In some cases – depending on where you live – ads in certain publications are free: try *Loot* in London or *FreeAds* in Kent and Surrey. You could also put an advertisement in a newsagent's window.

Car boot sales

Alternatively, you could sell at a car boot sale. If you haven't got a car, see if you can get someone with a car to help you. Car boot sales are held regularly in many areas, and the best way to find the ones near you is to contact your local council. Once you have found a car boot sale in your neighbourhood, go and check it out before you do your own. Check to see if it has attracted plenty of people: a busy car boot sale means more money for car booters. Entrance is usually free to shoppers, but as a car booter you will have to pay a small fee when you take your car full of goods there. However, you should be able to recoup the fee from what you sell. Make sure you check how much people are charging for items similar to your own, so that you'll have a good idea of how much to charge for your own items. Try also to remember the faces of people who are selling goods similar to yours: car-booters often buy things from other people at these sales and then sell them on at a higher price, so if you recognise a car booter among your customers, it may be an indication that you have priced your wares a little too low.

Although it's difficult to predict the weather, check out the weather forecasts in advance and try to pick a dry day if you can: many car boot sales take place in the open air, and rainy weather will deter some people. To get weather forecasts for up to five days ahead, look at the Teletext pages on television, or visit one of the weather websites on the internet, such as the Met Office at www.met-office.gov.uk/weather, or Yahoo weather on http://uk.weather.yahoo.com or the BBC weather site on www.bbc.co.uk/weather.

useful tip

Be prepared to haggle at car boot sales: some people really enjoy bargaining, and will offer you less no matter how low your price is. This is part of the fun, but if you're not confident about your haggling abilities, practise with a friend before you go, or ask someone else to haggle for you.

☒

On the day of the car boot sale, make sure you get there early so you can get a good position, and take a fold-up table with you so you can display as many of your things as possible. A wallpapering table – available from most DIY shops – is ideal as well as cheap, but borrowing one from a friend or relative is even cheaper.

A length of string tied tightly to each end of your car's boot – and some hangers – can provide a useful hanging rail for displaying a few clothes. Also pack a couple of plastic dust sheets, just in case it rains after all. Take some large boxes too: people enjoy rummaging through them, and they are useful for keeping lots of small items together. Make sure you have plenty of change to give to customers, and a supply of carrier bags ready.

Selling over the internet

Alternatively, why not try selling your goods over the internet? You can display them on a variety of websites, such as www.sell-all.co.uk. On this website you can advertise your items for sale in the same way as you would in a newspaper – simply state the price you are seeking. If you are a private advertiser, the advertisement is free, unless you are selling a car, caravan or house.

You can also put your items up for auction on the internet, but watch the small print: some auction sites say they are free, and although this may be true for buyers, sellers often have to pay a fee, usually a display fee or commission on the sale. By far the most popular internet auction site at the moment is eBay (www.ebay.co.uk). You can buy and sell anything on the site, from antiques to office goods and anything else besides. In fact, some people are running very successful businesses solely on eBay! For further details, see Useful addresses, page 203. To find other auction sites, simply key the words 'sell item auction uk' into your preferred search engine and you should have more sites at your fingertips. Remember to shop around and compare commission rates to ensure you are getting the best deal. Also, make sure you add on any commission fee to your reserve price before you start.

Internet sites come and go. You may also find that yesterday's free website now charges you for its services. Make sure, therefore, that you know exactly what the website charges before you use its services. Do regular checks through the search engines to locate new websites because new ones are more likely to offer their services for free, even if only for an introductory period.

When you have turned your clutter into cash, don't fritter it away: use it to help pay off your debts or invest it for later. Don't use it to fill your home with yet more clutter. Before buying an item, always ask yourself if you really need it and if you'll still be using it in a couple of years' time. If the answer is no to either of these questions, put it back on the shelf and walk out of the shop.

Finally, if you still have any items left over after all your sales are complete, don't be tempted to keep them. Donate them to a charity shop or jumble sale instead. Needy people will benefit from your generosity and you will have the satisfaction of knowing that you have done a good deed – in this way everyone wins.

4 CUTTING YOUR OUTGOINGS

The aim of this book is to show you that the road to financial freedom doesn't have to be harsh, and that you can still enjoy life while you're sorting out your finances. You'll learn in later chapters how you can have regular holidays, a good social life – or whatever it is that you enjoy best – for free or very little outlay. However, it is also vital to keep any unnecessary spending to a minimum while you're getting back on your feet.

Increasing your income is only half of the story: in order to wipe out your debts completely and make life more comfortable, you need to cut down on any unnecessary expenditure. This chapter is full of tips to help you get started.

Identify unnecessary spending

The first thing you need to do is have a close look at your spending and decide how much of it is necessary and how much of it you could do without. Even small things can mount up: for example, did you realise that if you buy a £1.20 coffee on the way to work each morning, it will actually cost you at least £24 a month? You could be using that £24 a month to help clear your debts. What about catching a bus for a short trip to and from the station every day?

Let's say it costs 50p each way: a 15-minute walk each way instead could save you at least £20 a month, and will help you get some exercise too. A 50p fare doesn't sound much, and neither does £1.00 a day, but working out how much it adds up to a month soon exposes the real cost.

Try doing this simple exercise with all the small items you pay for regularly. Newspapers, magazines, drinks, sweets and snacks, buses and taxis for short trips – these things really mount up when you count their cost over a month. If you buy these items daily, or even once a week, add up what they will cost you over a month. Then if you really want to shock yourself, work out how much they will cost you over a year. That innocent little coffee on the way to work each morning, for example, could cost you about £300 a year! If you cut out that coffee, the money you save could be used for something else. Just think how much you could save in interest if you used that money to pay off a credit card: interest on a balance of £300 can soon mount up – after five years that debt could have turned into thousands of pounds. This shows that even something as small as a daily coffee can have a really big impact on your finances. So identify the things you don't need, work out what they are really costing you, and cut them out.

The replacement technique

When you are identifying items to cut out of your expenditure, you may come across something that is not essential to life and limb, but without it you feel you would be unhappy or inconvenienced. So what do you do? For example, let's imagine you buy a newspaper every day. You may use it to help you keep track of the job market or your investments, or to follow the news for your business. On the other hand, you may buy it simply to enjoy reading it and you don't want to give up that pleasure. If it really would make you unhappy to go without it, then of course you should keep it. However, before you continue buying it at full price every day, why not try getting it much cheaper, or even for free? This is where my 'replacement technique' comes in.

The idea behind the replacement technique is simple: instead of cutting out the things you enjoy or would prefer not to be without, simply replace them with cheaper alternatives. In fact, you may find in many cases that you can replace an item with something that costs nothing at all.

Let's go back to the daily newspaper as an example. If you need your newspaper for your business, you may be able to get it supplied by your employer. If you are self-employed, you could ask your accountant about claiming an allowance against tax for it. If you need the newspaper for other reasons, such as to keep track of investments, help is still at hand. For example, if you need it solely to keep track of shares, you can check these for free using the Teletext or Ceefax pages on your television. These pages, and the regular television channels, are also an excellent source of all the latest news. Alternatively, if you have access to a computer, you can check the stock market via a number of websites, such as the Moneyextra website on www.moneyextra.com/stocks or the *Financial Times* website http://news.ft.com/yourmoney.

However, if you simply want to read a newspaper from cover to cover, you can do it for free on the internet. The *Guardian*, for example, is online: just click on www.guardian.co.uk to access its pages. The *Independent* is on www.independent.co.uk and *The Times* is on www.thetimes.co.uk. Remember, however, that the internet option works out cheaper only if you have free access to it, or if you have arranged to pay a set fee that gives you unlimited access so you do not increase your telephone bill every time you log on.

If you do not have access to the internet, try visiting your local library. Many libraries carry a set of daily newspapers, and reading a newspaper in the peace and quiet of a library can be a relaxing way to spend a lunchtime. Many libraries also give access to the internet, and some will let you log on for free, so it is certainly worth paying them a visit.

And what about that coffee in the mornings? If you feel that you really can't do without your morning dose of hot caffeine on the way to work, why not invest a few pounds in a vacuum flask and make your own coffee at home to take with you? The money you save will ensure that your flask pays for itself in around a week. Depending on the flask size, you could even get two or three coffees out of it, or tea if you prefer.

The same applies to snacks and lunches. Do you regularly fork out money for sweets and expensive sandwiches and cakes? This can amount to hundreds of pounds in a very short time. Try this tactic instead: go to a supermarket and buy what you would need for a week's worth of lunches and sweets. A loaf of bread and two or three different sandwich fillings, plus a bulk pack of assorted crisps or sweets, will cost a fraction of what you would pay in a café or sandwich shop over a week. If you incorporate buying your lunches into your weekly shopping, you could well find that most of the cost is absorbed into your weekly bill, and it will feel as if you are getting your lunches for free. If you have access to a microwave oven or toaster at work, so much the better. You will be able to eat more inventive meals, and save money into the bargain.

If you are tempted to say at this point, 'I never have time to make lunch in the mornings before I go to work', remember that you don't have to make it before you leave in the morning. You could make it the night before or, if necessary, just grab the bread and other ingredients, and make them up later, at lunchtime. You can save thousands of pounds doing this, and you will have the added benefit of knowing exactly what is going into your lunch – ideal if you are a vegetarian, on a calorie-controlled or low-fat diet, or need to watch the ingredients for some other reason.

The point of this exercise is to show you that you don't necessarily have to do without the things you enjoy: you just need to be inventive and find a cheaper way of getting them. So whenever you identify an expense like this, get into the habit of asking yourself, 'How can I cut the cost of this, or get it for free?'

The replacement technique is a very valuable method that you can use in every area of your life, as you will see later. In the meantime, simply concentrate on cutting down on your regular monthly outgoings, and see if you can use the replacement technique to save yourself more money. The financial statement you did in Chapter 1 (see page 8) should help with this: go over your outgoings and see if you can find free or cheaper replacements.

When I first used this method, I found all sorts of ways I could save money. For example, I used to belong to an expensive health club in London, where I attended aerobics classes, swam in the pool and jogged on treadmills. Using the replacement technique, I stopped my membership and instead started working out at home using aerobics videos, running around the neighbourhood and swimming in the local public pool. Nowadays I live near the sea, and have the option of swimming in the sea for free whenever I like, but I confess I still prefer the warmer temperature of a heated pool! However, for this I still use the local public swimming pool, which works out much cheaper. Eventually I treated myself to a compact treadmill with some of the money I had saved so that I could run indoors comfortably in rainy weather. The money I saved from making these changes has run into literally thousands of pounds.

Making savings

There are lots of ways you can make savings in daily life. Here are some ideas to get you started – see how many more of your own you can find, and put them into practice as soon as possible. Some of them you will be able to action straight away, but others may take a little time. Don't worry about this: just get started on the changes you can make immediately, and then chip away at the others until you have got everything for the best possible price.

ACCOMMODATION

Let's start with your accommodation costs. If you pay rent, are you paying too much? Have you checked that you are being charged a fair rent compared with similar properties in the neighbourhood? Or are you renting accommodation that is larger than you really need? Many people find themselves in this situation, especially after a relationship break-up or a friend moving out. Would downsizing help you to cut your monthly rent bill? Some people rent a home with an extra bedroom just so they can offer friends a room to sleep in when they visit. If this is you, move to a smaller place and give your friends a sofa bed in the lounge instead! Alternatively, why not let out that room? Remember the first £81.73 a week on that room is tax-free (see page 45), but don't forget to ask your landlord's permission before you sublet. What about the location of your home? Are you renting in a very expensive area? If so, could you move to a less expensive area and save money?

If you have a mortgage, do you know what its current interest rate is? Your mortgage may have been the best deal when you first took it out, but new and better deals come on to the market all the time. You may be able to save yourself a lot of money by asking your lender for a better rate or by switching to another lender. Shop around with at least three independent financial advisers until you find the best deal. Even though many financial advisers have access to the same products, in my experience they hardly ever seem to come up with the same ones. You can find independent financial advisers through many sources, such as the internet or estate agents, or through personal recommendation. Make sure you check the credentials of potential financial advisers thoroughly before you go ahead (see pages 150–1). Most estate agents have a financial adviser who will be happy to advise you, and the internet is full of brokers just waiting for the chance to give you a mortgage quotation.

Some websites offer online mortgage calculators. For example, if you want to borrow £80,000 and would like to find out how much it will cost per month, try logging on to the UK Mortgage Calculator on www.scientific.force9.co.uk/mortgage.htm and it will work it out for you. Alternatively, surf the net for other calculators – you'll have plenty of choice. However, remember that the point of this exercise is to reduce and eventually clear all your debt, so don't be tempted to remortgage for more money than you absolutely need.

Remember also to check the terms of your current mortgage: are there any early redemption penalties or other tie-ins? You may find, for instance, that you are tied into your mortgage arrangement for a certain number of years, and that if you pay off some or all of the loan before that time is up, you will incur a penalty of around three to six months' worth of instalments. This alone could amount to several thousand pounds. However, if you do find that there is a tie-in on your mortgage, all may not be lost. Your broker may still be able to find a deal that will save you money even after taking the redemption penalty into account.

GAS AND ELECTRICITY

What about your gas and electricity? Thanks to deregulation, you can now save hundreds of pounds a year by switching your gas and electricity suppliers. Competition for your business is fierce, and you will find a host of companies out there keen to supply your gas and electricity and offering cheaper deals to get you on board. When I switched my gas and electricity suppliers I saved over £300 a year. There is no fuss and no need to have an engineer round to change pipework or any installations, just a simple form to fill in; after about a month you will start receiving bills from the new company instead of the old one.

Deals vary around the country, however, and a company may be cheaper in one region yet more expensive in another. So don't take a company's word that it's the cheapest in your area; instead, shop around until you find the best deal. One of the quickest ways of doing this is to use a comparison website, such as www.buy.co.uk. Simply key in your postcode and a few other details, such as which company you're currently using and how much you pay over a year, and this site will tell you which is the cheapest company for you. You may find that it suggests one company for both your electricity and gas, or a different company for each of them. Either way, you could save a lot of money by switching suppliers now.

TELEPHONE CHARGES

You can make huge savings on your telephone bills. Let's take your land line first. There is a whole host of telephone companies out there just clamouring to offer you cheaper calls. Competition is fierce, and there is every chance that you will be able to save a lot of money by switching telephone companies. Contact the companies in your area and compare their charges. Remember to look at the charges for the calls you are most likely to make. If the only regular calls you make are to your parents in the next town, for instance, there is no point choosing a supplier that offers the cheapest prices for international calls but expensive rates for local calls. What time of day do you make most of your calls? Go through your past bills to get an idea of your telephone usage (if you've thrown them away, ask your existing telephone supplier to send you an itemised duplicate of the last one).

useful tip

Make sure that you're getting the cheapest deal for your water. Shop around between companies, and check you're getting the best deal by logging on to a comparison website such as www.buy.co.uk. To find other websites, key the words 'comparison utilities uk' into any internet search engine, and a list will appear at your fingertips.

Charges vary enormously between suppliers, and some will be more competitive on the type of call you make or if you telephone at certain times of day. The internet has a host of free websites that can compare telephone charges between different suppliers. Again the website www.buy.co.uk will help you compare charges, or try logging on to the Magenta Systems Limited website at www.magsys.co.uk/telecom, which compares a wide variety of residential and business tariffs. Whichever comparison site you use, I suggest that you choose three or four companies that offer a suitable service at the best price in your area, and then contact them direct to make sure their prices haven't changed since the site was last updated.

If there are several phone users in your household, and your phone bills are always large, you might want to consider a tariff that allows you to make unlimited calls for a fixed fee. For example, NTL currently operates a scheme that allows you to make unlimited calls to any numbers beginning 01- or 02- anywhere in the UK, 24 hours a day, 7 days a week, for £25 a month. The only proviso is that each call must be less than one hour's duration, or you will start to incur further charges. The scheme also offers lower rates for calls to mobile phones and international numbers. The market is changing all the time, however, and new deals are launched regularly, so shop around to find the cheapest and most suitable deal for you.

Currently you can also make free calls from your computer, as long as both you and the person you are calling have access to the internet.

You'll need headphones and a microphone – but you can do this for free using companies such as Skype. It also helps to have broadband, but this is not essential. For further information, see page 66.

useful tip

To compare mobile phone tariffs, log on to a comparison website such as www.buy.co.uk. If you do not have a computer, pop into your local mobile phone retailers and ask them to give you comparisons between the different tariffs available.

Competition between mobile phone companies is just as fierce. You'll be amazed at how much you can save each month by switching tariffs or suppliers. For example, I used to have a contract where I was paying £15 a month for line rental with charges for calls on top. Then I switched to a pay-as-you-go deal offered by a different company, and now pay no line rental at all. I simply pay in advance for £10 or £20 worth of calls, and then top it up whenever it gets low. This arrangement suits me because I don't make many calls from my mobile phone, but I do need to be able to receive calls when I'm out and about. I've already saved hundreds of pounds by switching to this deal. It is good value for money but it doesn't suit everyone; you may be better off with a different deal to suit your own circumstances. So make sure you have a good idea of the types of calls you make, how often you make them and at what time of day. Then shop around to find the best deal for you. It may take some time to work your way through the large number of deals on offer, but the savings will be worth it.

INSURANCE

You can save literally thousands of pounds by shopping around for cheaper insurance policies. You need to make sure, of course, that the policy offers the right type of cover for you, and be aware of any exclusions in the policy. You should also be aware of any excesses you would be required to pay in the event of a claim. Check that you are buying insurance at the correct level for your needs: many people are under- or over-insured, which can be expensive or cause problems later if they need to make a claim. So go through all your insurance needs, then look for the best deal. To get you started, here are a few you might like to check:

- Life insurance
- Home contents insurance
- Buildings insurance
- Motor vehicle insurance
- Health insurance
- Travel insurance
- Critical illness/income protection insurance
- Pet insurance

By the time you've worked your way through all your insurance needs and found the best possible prices, you will have saved yourself a huge amount of money. For example, by switching my car insurer this year I halved my annual premium *and* got Green Flag roadside vehicle recovery thrown in for free. This enabled me to cancel my AA road-side vehicle recovery membership and save myself a further £156 a year. So get busy on the internet, or if you're not online, choose a handful of insurance brokers from your local telephone book and ask them to find the best deal available. It doesn't hurt to let them know you are shopping around

useful tip

Try logging on to www. easy-quote.co.uk, which offers a free insurance quotation service. This site covers a wide range of insurers to make shopping around as easy as possible, ranging from home contents, motor vehicles, health and travel to business insurance policies. You can also compare insurance quotes on the website www.buy.co.uk.

– it will provide an added incentive for them to track down the best deal on your behalf.

OTHER FINANCIAL SERVICES

What about your pension plan – are you getting the best deal? And do you know the interest rates you are paying on your loans and any hire purchase agreements? Moving your borrowing to a cheaper lender could save you a fortune in interest, but remember to look out for any early redemption penalties. If you do move your borrowing, do not be tempted to borrow more than you currently owe. The object of this exercise is to reduce your debt, not increase it.

Also try logging on to the *Financial Times* website mentioned earlier, http://news.ft.com/yourmoney. In addition to clear explanations on matters ranging from choosing your insurance to how the stock market works, this site allows you to compare different companies' quotations for pensions, insurance, mortgages, personal loans and utilities such as gas and electricity, and buy online. You can even check the latest share prices.

TRAVEL

How do you get around? Are you getting the best value for money when you travel? You can make a lot of savings here. Try walking instead of catching the bus or train for short journeys. If your children's school is within walking distance, walk with them there instead of taking them by bus or car. The exercise will do you good, and it will give you a chance to spend a bit more time with your kids.

If you drive, where do you buy your petrol? Petrol sold on motorways or in out-of-the-way places is often more expensive than petrol sold in other areas, such as in towns and cities. Try shopping around, and if you find a supplier that regularly sells cheaper petrol, fill up there whenever you can. Some garages, especially those run by supermarkets, give incentives such as loyalty cards with 'points' that you can save and get free gifts or money off your shopping. These can be useful, but make sure that the garage is not charging you more for your petrol in order to give you these incentives.

Keep your car well maintained to make sure that it isn't using too much petrol. Switching to a car with a smaller engine capacity can also save you money on your insurance premiums and vehicle licence costs. If you make regular journeys to and from work, why not join a car share scheme or start one in your area? You could also start one with colleagues and share the cost of travelling to and from work.

If you use buses or trains, seek out the best deals. Buying a monthly season ticket could save you money, and travelling during off-peak times could reduce the price significantly. Ask the ticket clerk for the cheapest deals available.

If your journeys are within cycling distance, why not invest in a bicycle? Leaving a little earlier and cycling along quieter routes or on roads with bike lanes is safer and can be very enjoyable. Cycling is also a very beneficial form of exercise. Joining a cycling club can be rewarding too, and could help you make new friends. You might even get your loved ones hooked, and you could go for outings and picnics together. In time, the money you save from cycling instead of paying for bus and train fares will more than pay for the cost of the bicycle.

You don't even need to pay full price for a bicycle. Try picking one up at an online auction instead. Simply key the words 'buy auction uk' into an internet search engine such as Yahoo or Google, and a number of auction sites will be at your fingertips. Many of them are free to buyers, but check the small print, just in case. If you are not online, you can also buy bicycles that come from reputable sources such as liquidated stocks from auctions around the country. The police also regularly auction bicycles from their stock of lost property and recovered goods. See pages 204–5 for examples of auction houses that sell cheap bicycles.

FOOD BILLS

You can make enormous savings on your food bills. Simply changing where you shop can save you hundreds of pounds a year. There can be as much as £20 to £40 difference on a trolley of similar items bought from different supermarkets in one week in my area. Worked out over a year, that could amount to as much as £2,080 saved, depending on where I shop.

Where do you do the bulk of your food shopping? It's time to find out which shops in your area offer the most competitive prices. Try this exercise and see for yourself. Make a list of the items you buy every week, such as bread, milk, butter or margarine, cooking oil, potatoes and other vegetables, fruit, eggs and so on. Then turn it into a chart, like this:

Item	Shop A	Shop B	Shop C	Shop D
Loaf of bread				
Pint of milk				
Pat of butter				
Potatoes (per 450g/1lb)				
Tomatoes (per 450g/1lb)				
Mushrooms (per 450g/1lb)				
Eggs (per dozen)				
Baked beans (per 200g/7oz tin)				
Oranges (each)				
Total (£):				

It is not necessary to keep to the quantities suggested here, but once you have decided on a quantity and size, you should stick to it in each shop. You should also keep to the same brand or compare equivalent own-brand items between your chosen shops. In that way, you will be able to compare like for like. You don't need to list everything you buy each week, but the more items you include, the more accurate your chart will be, so try to include a good selection.

When you have your chart ready, choose four different shops or supermarkets. Try to pick at least one shop or supermarket that you believe to be the cheapest, even if it's a little further away than the shop you usually use. Also ask your friends and neighbours which ones they use and/or believe to be the cheapest. Make sure you include the shop you normally use. Then take your chart to each of the four shops and mark on it the prices charged by each one. When you have finished, add up each column and write the totals in the spaces provided. Then compare the figures. You may be very surprised at the differences between them. Only in this way can you be sure you are getting the best deal.

If you are used to shopping at an expensive shop, you may feel concerned about the quality of food available at a cheaper shop. Let me reassure you here. If you shop at any one of the major supermarkets, you can be sure that their products will come up to an acceptable standard. Some food items do vary, of course, such as fresh fruit and vegetables, and you may find that you prefer the apples from one particular supermarket. If you find that the fresh fruit and vegetables are not as good from the cheaper store, or go off too quickly, then by all means buy them from your preferred source. That doesn't have to stop you buying other products from the cheaper store, however. Brand name items will be of a similar quality everywhere, so your tin of Heinz baked beans will be of the same quality whether you buy it from the most expensive shop or from the cheapest one. Products such as toilet rolls, kitchen foil, tissues and cleaning products will all be of an acceptable quality in the cheaper shop. Many supermarkets' 'own brand' items, such as tinned tomatoes, are good too. In fact, in some cases, these own brand products may actually be the same products as the branded ones, but just packaged differently and sold at a lower price. You can also use internet comparison tables, such as www.trollydolly.co.uk, to help you cut your shopping costs, but use these with care, since relevant information featured on these sites may be limited. Always back up your research by visiting the shops in person.

⭐

useful tip

Never go shopping for food on an empty stomach! You'll be tempted to buy things that were not on your original list. Eat before you go, have a shopping list ready and stick to it.

⭐

Remember that buying ready-made meals will really push up your food costs. Although they are convenient, they are very expensive and often not even satisfying. They may be full of artificial additives too. Next time you are out shopping, try to avoid buying these items. Opt instead for fresh ingredients you can prepare yourself. Preparing and cooking fresh, simple meals need not be time-consuming, and it can save you a fortune over a year. There are many good cookbooks available to give you ideas for delicious meals that are quick to make and easy on your budget. If you can't afford to buy books, try your local library. Supermarkets also give away free printed recipe cards from time to time.

Stacking up the savings

I could not finish this chapter on money saving without mentioning Martin Lewis, the UK's acknowledged money-saving expert. If you have access to the internet, you will not regret logging on to his website at www.moneysavingexpert.com. Through Martin my partner and I have flown to Spain for a fortnight and back for the princely sum of four pence; I have had a free meal for four in a Japanese restaurant, and the pleasure of a credit card company paying *me* £250, at no cost to me. I have even cut the cost of parking at airports, and get driven from my car to the terminal and back for free. If, like me, you have a lot of demands on your time, you will find his site invaluable for giving you the current cheapest deals on *anything* at the click of a mouse. He even shows you how to make telephone calls on your computer for free. He has also written an excellent money-saving book called *The Money Diet* (see Further reading, page 211).

You should find, at the end of all this, that you have saved yourself a fortune on your monthly costs. Why not try adding up your savings over a month, and then multiplying them by 12 to find out how much you will save over the coming year? You may discover that you have saved yourself thousands of pounds, and can congratulate yourself for a job well done.

If this list of money-saving ideas seems long or overwhelming, remember that you don't need to do it all at once. If necessary, tackle one item at a time, and then deal with another when you next have time. In order to make the most savings, however, you should aim to get through the whole list in a reasonably short time. Ideally, go through this list again at least once a year, because prices change and you need to make sure you continue to get the best deals. Some insurance companies, for instance, push up their premiums from time to time and rely on customers' loyalty or lethargy for them not to switch companies and get a better deal elsewhere. Be disloyal! Don't pay more than is absolutely necessary. Keep informed and make sure you stay aware of all the best deals so that you can switch and save yourself a fortune whenever possible. The potential savings, and your increased peace of mind, will be worth it.

5 SPY ON YOUR SPENDING

Do you sometimes find that your money seems to disappear into invisible 'holes', even when you have watched every penny and done all the sums? That no matter how hard you try, and how accurately you have budgeted, your money has melted away into thin air? Well, you're in good company, because everyone I know has experienced this phenomenon at some point in their lives.

Often it is difficult to know exactly where every penny goes – extra costs have a way of slipping in and catching you unawares. It is as if the gremlins are helping themselves to your money, and no amount of budgeting can stop them.

If you find yourself in this situation after all the budgeting and planning you have been doing earlier in this book – and you probably will – then the time has come to plug all those invisible money leaks. You need to start spying on your own spending, and the easiest way to do this is to keep a money diary.

Your money diary doesn't have to be an elaborate affair: you can buy a cheap diary or notebook that has enough room to enter your spending for each day, or you can recycle sheets of paper and keep clipping them together. It doesn't matter what you use, as long as you write all your spending into it every day. Even if you buy a packet of chewing gum, this has to go into the diary. I know this sounds extreme, but bear with me on this because only by writing everything down will you be able to see where your money is really going – how much of it, and how often. You will at last see your true spending habits, and they may surprise you!

Starting a money diary

The most important thing to remember about keeping a money diary is that you must get into the habit of using it every day. If you don't, you won't get a true picture of your spending, and those money leaks will stay hidden. Writing all your spending into your diary every day will bring those leaks to light, so that you can identify and put a stop to them. To get the best results, you should keep the diary going for a minimum of six weeks, but three or four months would be even better. The longer you keep your money diary, the better chance you will have of catching all those expenses, including any quarterly bills you may have forgotten.

Your diary should show the day and date, and have enough space to write, say, a dozen lines underneath. An example of a blank money diary is given on page 81. Showing the day of the week is important because in this way you can see at a glance if you tend to spend more money on certain days than others. You may spend more on Saturdays, for example, by going out shopping and then socialising in the evening. When you know this about yourself, you can be prepared and look for ways to reduce your spending on those particular days.

When you have set up your diary, take it with you everywhere you go, and write in it absolutely everything you spend. Every time you write a cheque, use a debit or credit card or pay cash for something, even if it's for only a few pence, write it in the diary. If you are rushed and haven't got time to write in an entry, add it at the very first opportunity afterwards. For example, if you buy a book and then have to rush to catch a train, keep the receipt, and write the amount into your diary as soon as you have settled into your seat on the train.

Your entries do not have to be long; in fact, keeping them short will be less of a chore and will encourage you to keep the diary going. Simply write a brief description of the item and how much it cost. Remember, however, that you do need to list every item separately. For example, if you have just bought some breakfast for yourself on the way to work, write it down as follows:

Toast	£1.00
Coffee	£1.50

Don't be tempted to summarise by writing 'Breakfast £2.50'. Likewise, if you have just bought some cosmetics, don't write 'Cosmetics £17.00'. You will need to separate them out, as follows:

Shower gel	£3.50
Shampoo	£3.00
Hair conditioner	£3.00
Body lotion	£5.00
Hand cream	£2.50

Separating things out in this way is essential if you are going to be able to look back through your diary and pinpoint exactly what you're spending your money on.

You should also include any unexpected bills. For example, if you have just had to spend £35.00 getting a new wing mirror for your car, write it in your diary as soon as you have written out your cheque. The only things you don't need to include in your money diary are your regular living expenses that get paid by direct debit or standing order and which you've already included in your personal chart. For example, if you pay your rent or mortgage by direct debit, then you will already have a note of this and there is no need to write it in your diary. But if you pay your rent by cheque,

I suggest you do include it in your money diary, so that every time you write a cheque it becomes automatic for you to reach for your diary.

THE MONEY DIARY IN ACTION

Here is an example of a money diary. It contains entries for a typical week's spending by Joan, whose personal finance chart we saw in Chapter 1 (see page 4). She is divorced, with a young daughter called Sarah. Joan is very organised and pays her rent and regular bills by standing order and direct debit from her bank account, so she needs to enter only what she pays for by cash, cheque, or debit or credit card.

MONDAY 6 MARCH

Item	Cost (£)
Adult weekly bus pass	17.50
Child weekly bus pass	7.50
Sandwich (Joan)	2.50
Sarah's pocket money	2.50
Total	**30.00**

TUESDAY 7 MARCH

Item	Cost (£)
Sandwich (Joan)	2.50
Chocolate bar (Joan)	0.50
Total	**3.00**

WEDNESDAY 8 MARCH

Item	Cost (£)
Sandwich (Joan)	2.50
Adult swimming class	3.50
Child swimming class	2.50
Two teas after swimming	3.00
Total	**11.50**

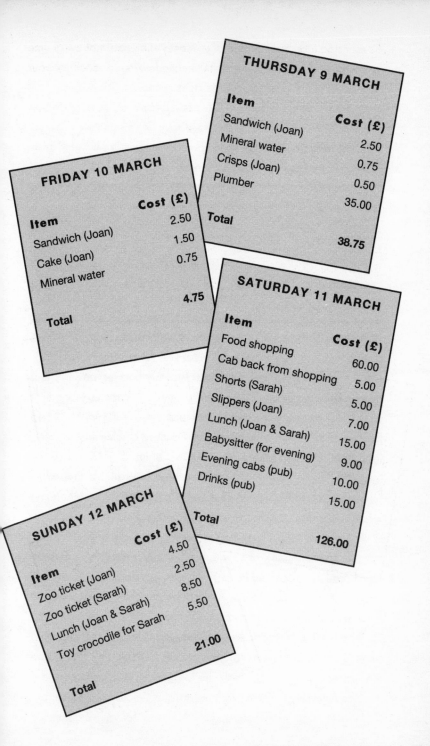

THURSDAY 9 MARCH

Item	Cost (£)
Sandwich (Joan)	2.50
Mineral water	0.75
Crisps (Joan)	0.50
Plumber	35.00
Total	**38.75**

FRIDAY 10 MARCH

Item	Cost (£)
Sandwich (Joan)	2.50
Cake (Joan)	1.50
Mineral water	0.75
Total	**4.75**

SATURDAY 11 MARCH

Item	Cost (£)
Food shopping	60.00
Cab back from shopping	5.00
Shorts (Sarah)	5.00
Slippers (Joan)	7.00
Lunch (Joan & Sarah)	15.00
Babysitter (for evening)	9.00
Evening cabs (pub)	10.00
Drinks (pub)	15.00
Total	**126.00**

SUNDAY 12 MARCH

Item	Cost (£)
Zoo ticket (Joan)	4.50
Zoo ticket (Sarah)	2.50
Lunch (Joan & Sarah)	8.50
Toy crocodile for Sarah	5.50
Total	**21.00**

As you can see from Joan's diary, she tends to do most of her spending at weekends. She doesn't spend so much during weekdays when she is at work, but she does spend £2.50 every day on a sandwich, and some days she has extras, such as a packet of crisps, a cake or a drink. Now these may seem innocent enough, but if we total up what she spends on her lunches from Monday to Friday, we can see the figures more clearly:

Monday:	£ 2.50
Tuesday:	£ 3.00
Wednesday:	£ 2.50
Thursday:	£ 3.75
Friday:	£ 4.75
Total:	£16.50

This £16.50 she spends each week actually adds up to £71.50 a calendar month (£16.50 x 52 weeks ÷ 12 months = £71.50). None of it has been included in her monthly budget, and this is a good example of how those invisible money leaks can begin. It would be very easy for Joan to replace these items with packed lunches because she already makes a packed lunch every morning for Sarah to take to school. She could save a further £3 a week by taking a flask of tea on Wednesday swimming nights instead of buying teas afterwards. In fact, simply replacing the tea alone would more than pay for Sarah's swimming class each week.

The bulk of Joan's spending, however, is at weekends. It's nice to eat out occasionally, of course, but if money is tight, the zoo lunch could easily be replaced by a picnic. Joan could also split the cost of her Saturday night cabs with a friend, or halve the cab costs by catching a bus there and a cab back.

So it is clear that Joan needs to add other items to her personal finance chart. She needs to allow for her outings with Sarah and the occasional present, which she forgot to add in before. And if she has a weekly meal out with Sarah, she should add that in too.

Finally, Joan should make an allowance for any unexpected

bills, such as the plumber who was needed on the Thursday when her washing machine sprang a leak. These expenses are difficult to estimate in advance, so I suggest making a calculated guess at first, and then adjusting the amount when more accurate figures are available from the diary over a period of time. She could decide to allow, for example, £40 a month for unexpected costs. If she doesn't use the money, she can then keep it for any larger bills that may arise later in the year. In this way, she is giving herself added protection against any financial emergencies.

Make spying a habit

If you can get into the habit of keeping your money diary going for as long as possible – at least several months – you will get an even more accurate picture. This will enable you to identify your spending patterns over a longer period. You may find, for example, that all goes to plan for three-and-a-half months, and then suddenly a £150 bill arrives for car repairs. Only by keeping a money diary regularly can you be absolutely sure where every penny is being spent. And if you manage to take the bull by the horns and keep your diary for a whole year, you will find it even easier to budget accurately for the future. Simply pick out all the unexpected bills for the year, total them up, and then divide by 12 to give you an average monthly cost (or divide by 52 to give you a weekly amount). In Joan's case, this would work as follows:

July:	Plumber	35.00
November:	TV repairs	55.00
January:	Electrician	155.00
March:	Broken window	65.00
June:	Oven repair	90.00
	Total:	**£400.00**

(divide the total of £400 by 12 = £33.33 per month)

If Joan had allowed £40 per month to cover all her unexpected household bills, she would have found herself with £80 left over at the end of the year, which she could have spent on a treat or saved for a rainy day. Over that first year the unexpected bills worked out at £33.33 per month, but since money is tight I suggest leaving the amount at £40 per month over the following year too, just in case. After year two, if Joan finds that she has even more money left over, then perhaps she could reduce the monthly amount slightly, to say £36 or £37. Remember, however, that costs of labour and materials go up with inflation, so it will be necessary to allow an increasing amount for these kinds of bills each year.

As with all good systems, the key to making them work is to know yourself. There is no point trying to stick to a regime that you know you are not going to be able to keep up. If you know, therefore, that you are not going to manage to keep a money diary over a whole year, or even for a few months, then try to do so for at least six to eight weeks in order to give yourself a reasonable idea of where your money is going. Then repeat the exercise at least once a year, for six to eight weeks at a time, just to keep an eye on things, because circumstances can change and your spending habits may vary from one year to the next. However, if your lifestyle is so hectic that you can't be sure you'll be able to keep the diary for even six weeks, then keeping it going for even a week or two will give you a better idea of where the holes are in your pocket, as long as you pick typical and not exceptional weeks. On the opposite page is a sample of a blank money diary for you to copy and fill in.

MONEY DIARY

MONDAY	/ /		FRIDAY	/ /
item	cost(£)		item	cost(£)

TUESDAY	/ /		SATURDAY	/ /
item	cost(£)		item	cost(£)

WEDNESDAY	/ /
item	cost(£)

SUNDAY	/ /
item	cost(£)

THURSDAY	/ /
item	cost(£)

Controlling your spending

If, after having done all this, you find a bewildering amount of entries in your diary, or you simply know that you're spending far more than you should be, the time has come to take a long, hard look at yourself and your spending habits. What is causing you to overspend? Perhaps you love shopping and find it hard to resist whatever takes your fancy, or you find it difficult not to be over-generous when you're out with friends. Do you keep buying large rounds of drinks, for instance? Or perhaps it's a case of priorities: some people baulk at the thought of spending £30 on a theatre ticket, but think nothing of spending £40 to £50 a night in a pub or club.

You need to get to know your spending habits and what your priorities are. Look at the reasons why you spend and how you feel when you are buying things.

Some people have emotional reasons for spending money. They get addicted to the emotional high of making a purchase – it makes them feel more in control. Some people take control of their relationship with their partner by doing all the spending, while others are compulsive gamblers or hooked on telephone chat-lines.

If any of this sounds familiar to you, or your spending has become a compulsion for whatever reason, you need to get some professional advice and support as soon as possible. It is vital that you tackle your need to overspend immediately, or you won't be able to stick to any financial plans or arrangements you make with creditors. Long-term private counselling is expensive, so talk to your GP about it – he or she may be able to refer you somewhere you can get counselling for free. If you prefer to find your own counsellor, make sure that he or she is suitably qualified and that you feel comfortable talking to that person. If you don't, try somewhere else.

Some organisations offer free counselling, advice, information or support to help people understand their spending habits and bring them under control. In the first instance try the Consumer Credit Counselling Service (see Useful addresses, page 194). They keep a list of counsellors and organisations that can help you for free, no matter what the reasons are behind your overspending. From compulsive shopping and addictions such as gambling to complex personal relationships, they will usually know of an organisation that can help you.

FORMING A BATTLE PLAN

While you are learning to change your spending habits, here are some emergency tactics you can use to help you avoid spending money when you are out and about:

- Leave your chequebook, credit cards and debit cards at home, and take cash with you instead. Cash feels more like real money and is harder to part with.

- If you are worried about spending too much cash, take out only a very small amount, say £5, and leave the rest at home.

- Keep away from shops. Visit a friend or relative instead, or head for the park, countryside or beach and have a walk or a picnic.

- If you simply have to buy something, only allow yourself to go to a jumble sale and restrict yourself to buying one item for under £3.

- Don't window shop. This only fuels the desire to buy.

- Stay away from advertising on the television and in magazines and newspapers as much as you can.

- Don't believe the marketing hype that tells you you'll be more beautiful or successful if you buy a certain product. Learn to insulate yourself against it and recognise the hype for what it is.

- If you know you spend to get an emotional high or to ease depression, try doing something else to lift your spirits. Take up a sport or hobby, for example, or watch a comedy on the television – anything you enjoy that will help cheer you up.

OVERSPENDING ON OTHER PEOPLE

Sometimes the reasons we overspend aren't so much to do with clever advertising and pampering ourselves, but because we are over-spending on other people. Human relationships can involve all kinds of complicated emotions, and these often get tied up with finances.

Paying for friends

Do you have a friend who never has any money? Do you ever ask that person out, knowing in advance that your friend is going to say he or she doesn't have any money and that you will end up paying for you both? If a friend is broke, then of course there is no harm in treating him or her to a trip out once in a while. But if this turns into a habit, then the relationship has become one-sided, and you could find yourself in the position where you are always expected to pay. If you are living together, the situation could be much worse. You may find yourself paying the lion's share of the household expenses, and sooner or later this is going to cause resentment.

Although being hard up is not necessarily your friend's fault, you shouldn't have to shoulder the responsibility of supporting him or her. Outings, for example, are not essential to life, and if your friend is regularly letting you pay for them, then this is bound to put an unnecessary burden on your finances.

You should be particularly wary of paying for expensive outings. Regular trips to bars and clubs, for instance, usually involve paying for expensive drinks and perhaps entrance fees. Meals in restaurants or regular takeaways also stretch the finances very quickly. If all this is sounding familiar, then you need to take action before things spiral out of control.

There is no need to fall out with your friend, but it's important to start looking after yourself too. If you live together and he or she isn't contributing towards the household expenses, gently explain that you are getting into debt and can't afford the same level of spending anymore, and that he or she will need to make a contribution from now on. Suggest a weekly figure, and make sure it takes into account things that are often easy to overlook, such as toilet rolls, cleaning products, tea, coffee and milk. When it comes to treats, try the replacement technique I outlined in Chapter 4 (see pages 56–9). In other words, replace going to expensive places such as bars and clubs with cheaper options that don't put a drain in your pocket, such as walks and picnics in the countryside, or visiting a free exhibition or museum. You could also have get-togethers with friends in your home or go to theirs. In the next chapter you will find more detailed information on many outings you can have for free, and other leisure ideas that are very cheap indeed.

If your friend is a true friend and really cares about your well-being and peace of mind, he or she should have no problem with your suggestions. You should find your friend making every effort to help, even if the weekly contribution towards household expenses takes a few weeks to sort out. In the meantime, however, there should be no resistance to the changes in outings. If you do encounter an unhelpful or uncooperative attitude, then it is time you looked at your relationship more closely because it will be obvious that your friend has started to use you and does not have your best interests at heart. Remember that you are just as important as other people and that you are worth protecting and caring for, so don't let other people take advantage of you.

Looking at the other side of the coin, some people press money on their friends and insist on paying for everything. In these cases, even making simple purchases like a bottle of wine or a few cans of beer can turn into a battle. If you find that you are insisting on paying all the time, take a back seat and let your friend have an equal say in the relationship. You can't buy friendship, and your friend will think no less of you for letting him or her pay for things on an equal basis.

Fair and equal partnerships

Having equal relationships applies just as much to partners. If you feel that you are shouldering too much of the financial responsibility in your relationship, you need to discuss it openly and put it right before it ruins your relationship as well as your finances. Disagreeing about money is one of the main causes of divorce and relationship breakdown in this country; the best way to avoid it is by dealing with it now rather than ignoring it and letting the resentment build up. If necessary, get some professional advice or counselling. Start by contacting the Consumer Credit Counselling Service (see Useful addresses, page 194).

Pampering children

There is often a great temptation to overindulge your children or someone else's, especially if the parents have broken up. Showering gifts of toys or money on children is no substitute for love, friendship and support, and it can create unhealthy expectations as well as additional responsibilities. It is better to concentrate on sharing quality time with children by having fun with them, playing games and listening to their needs, rather than overindulging and spoiling them with presents they don't need.

If you suspect an underlying problem is destabilising your finances, such as a relationship problem or an addiction of some kind, and you want to get expert help, the Consumer Credit Counselling Service (see Useful addresses, page 194) keep a list of qualified counsellors and other professionals who can help you for free.

6 REWARD YOURSELF

Getting out of debt doesn't have to mean cutting back all the time and not having any fun. You can still have a great time and enjoy all the good things in life, even while your finances recover.

What is your idea of a good life? Naturally we all have different ideas here. Some of you may instantly think of relaxing holidays abroad or fun days out with the family, while others may prefer dressing in glamorous designer clothes and going to parties and nightclubs. Whichever way of life suits you best, there is usually a way to get it without spending a fortune. In fact, in many cases you can have what you want for free.

To get you started, this chapter concentrates on some popular leisure activities, and looks into some of the ways you can get the most from them without making a hole in your budget. Here you will find helpful suggestions on how to cut the cost of eating and drinking with friends, and how to keep travel costs down. We will then move on to explore how you, your family and friends can enjoy a vast range of free leisure activities all around the country, including days out and entertainment. There really is no need to pay anything at all – you can have free days out as often as you like. In Chapter 10 you will find information on how to get a wide range of other things for free, or for very little outlay, from exciting holidays in the UK and abroad to designer clothes and many other luxury items.

Socialising on a budget

A good social life should be within everyone's reach, and you shouldn't have to break the bank for it. All you need to do is make a few adjustments, and where necessary use the replacement technique outlined in Chapter 4 (see pages 56–9). If your idea of a good time involves having drinks or dinner with friends, for example, why not meet up in each other's homes occasionally, instead of going to expensive restaurants or bars? Entertaining at home doesn't have to be expensive. If you decide to throw a party, for example, ask everyone to bring a bottle and some party food such as crisps, or throw the party with a friend so that you can share the expense. If you need party music, try to borrow it from a friend or relative.

If you decide to have a dinner party, plan your menu well in advance so you can choose recipes that are economical to prepare and keep shopping costs to a minimum. Avoid dishes that require a long list of exotic or expensive ingredients – choose fresh, simple fare instead. Buy ingredients that you can prepare yourself – carrots, for example, will be less expensive if you buy them whole and unpeeled. In fact, most vegetables and salad ingredients will work out cheaper if you wash, peel, trim and slice them yourself. You will also find there are many helpful books that will show you how to prepare and cook impressive, delicious meals on a budget. You can buy these books cheaply from supermarkets or, even better, borrow them for free from your local library.

When you decide to go out, spending a few minutes beforehand seeking out reasonably priced establishments will save you a fortune later. When you are in a pub or bar, choose cheaper drinks, or share the cost of drinks with your friends by suggesting a whip-round. Also look out for cheaper drinks during 'happy hours'. If you go on to one particular nightclub regularly, it may be possible for you to take out a membership and save money on entrance fees. And whenever you decide to eat out, look for special deals. For example, if you can time your visit for late afternoon instead of early evening, you may be able to take advantage of extended cheaper lunchtime prices. Some restaurants also offer discounts on certain days or nights of the week.

Finally, remember that arranging your transport home in advance will help you avoid hiring expensive cabs on the spur of the moment – perhaps you could get a lift from someone, share the transport cost with a friend or arrange to stay the night at the home of a relative or friend? The key to all this is planning: as soon as you know what you will be doing and when, take the time to do a little research and make a simple plan beforehand, and you will save yourself a lot of money.

Getting out and about

When it comes to outings and days out, you will be amazed at just how much there is to do in your area either very cheaply or for free. Why not join a conservation charity? The National Trust, for example, is a registered charity that was founded in 1895 to preserve places of historic interest or natural beauty. It protects and maintains over 300 historic houses and gardens around the UK and preserves not only 612,000 acres of the most beautiful countryside, but also 600 miles

useful tip

When eating out in restaurants, keep an eye on your drinks. Drinks prices are often not shown on menus in restaurant windows, and they can really push up your bill. Even water can be expensive. If you don't mind drinking tap water, ask for a jug of this instead of bottled water – this can make a big difference to your bill. And if you have any wine left, ask the restaurant staff to put a cork in the bottle so that you can take it home. You can also take home your leftover food. Many people do, so don't be afraid to ask.

of outstanding coastline. You can enjoy the tranquillity of lakes, waterfalls, bluebell woods and beautiful gardens, and feel history come alive as you explore the National Trust's beautiful houses and stately homes. Membership gives you memorable days out at a wide range of stunning properties and sites, and the satisfaction of knowing that your money is helping to protect our heritage. At the time of writing, annual membership costs £38.00 per adult, £63.50 for a couple or £68.50 for a family group – in this case a family is classed as two adults living at the same address, plus children or grandchildren under 18 years of age. The number of children allowed in is usually around three, but this is discretionary and many properties allow more. There are also discounts if you pay by direct debit. Annual membership entitles you to free entry and parking at all of their buildings and sites, and a free handbook giving details of all their properties, including opening times and maps. So once you have paid your annual membership fee, you can pack in as many free visits to their properties as you like. The National Trust also supplies full information about access for disabled people.

The National Trust is not the only organisation that preserves buildings and land for the nation. There are others, such as English Heritage. To contact The National Trust or English Heritage, see Useful addresses, page 191. You can also find other organisations on the internet.

But why pay anything at all for your days out? If you prefer to keep your money firmly in your pocket, there are countless things you can do for free all around the country. Your nearest tourist information centre can give you lots of useful information about places to go and things to see that won't cost you a penny. Wherever you are, whether you are at home or travelling, there is always something to do. To give you an idea of just how much is out there, I have chosen seven cities around the UK and looked into some of the things you can do for free in and around those places. There are too many to fit in here, so what follows is a small selection to whet your appetite.

LONDON: OUTINGS FOR FREE

This huge and fascinating city is well known for being expensive, but it is absolutely full of things you can do for free. In fact, there are so many that Harden's Guides have produced a book on them called *London For Free*. This immensely useful guide has over 160 pages packed with helpful information on beautiful parks, ancient woodlands, famous museums and galleries, spectacular events, memorable entertainments and many other free attractions. It also includes some very helpful maps and reviews. It is available from bookshops or direct from Harden's (see Useful addresses, page 198). Whatever your age or interests, whether you are a local resident or a visitor, you don't need to part with a penny to enjoy yourself in this great city.

Why not start with a walk by the lake through beautiful **St James's Park**, with its many species of colourful birds and equally exotic tourists? If you time your walk through the park to arrive at **Buckingham Palace** a little after 11am, you will be able to see the **Changing the Guard** ceremony, which takes place daily between April and October, and every other day between November and March.

Then why not enjoy the thrill of an auction? Two of London's most famous auction houses, **Christie's** and **Sotheby's**, give free admission to onlookers. You are welcome to look at the items to be auctioned beforehand and to attend the ensuing sale – an exciting show in itself. Or how about a visit to a **television studio** to watch a show being filmed? An enormous choice of quiz programmes, debates, comedies and other shows are recorded during the day and in the evening. Simply apply to the television company in advance and you will receive free tickets. Contact details for the BBC and ITV are given in Useful addresses, pages 196 and 198.

London boasts a huge range of museums and art galleries, and you can get into many of them for free. The **British Museum**, for example, will keep you busy for days, so it is probably best to tackle it section by section according to what interests you most. The

Although every effort has been made to ensure that details of the venues and events listed in this book are correct, opening times and venues do change from time to time. For example, some buildings close temporarily for renovation works, so you should always check that your chosen building is open, or that an event is definitely going ahead, before you go there.

★

collection of Egyptian antiquities is one of the most famous: it includes imposing statues and a vast range of coins, jewellery and other treasures.

The **Tate Britain** gallery at Millbank contains a huge collection of art, and you will find many of the most famous British artists since 1500 represented there. South of the Thames, **Tate Modern** houses one of the world's largest collections of modern and contemporary art since 1900, and represents all the major movements from Fauvism onwards.

If music is your passion, major arts centres such as the **Royal Festival Hall**, the **National Theatre** and the **Royal Opera House** regularly offer free foyer music. Also, large music stores and bookshops such as HMV, Virgin Records, and Borders host live performances and concerts occasionally. You can find details of other free musical events in *Time Out* magazine.

Free events take place all over London throughout the year, including festivals and parades, exhibitions, firework displays, marathons and regattas, and many more. Ask for details of these at your nearest tourist information centre.

Finally, when travelling around London, remember that although it is a large city, many attractions are located in central London and can be reached quite easily on foot. Even places that seem far apart on the Underground tube map may be closer than you think. For example, it takes only 45 minutes to walk from Covent Garden to Camden Town, and a little less to walk from Blackfriars to Oxford

Circus. So before you buy a ticket to travel by bus or tube, consider doing the journey on foot instead. It's a healthy and free way to travel, and you will enjoy all the beautiful sights and sounds that travellers on the Underground miss.

PLYMOUTH: EXCITING FREE ATTRACTIONS

The West Country is full of areas of outstanding beauty and wonderful things you can do for free, and I have chosen Plymouth to give you an idea of some of the things that are available in that region. This outstanding city by the sea is well placed for a whole host of exciting activities, with its combination of sea, rivers, moors and stunning countryside. Walkers are particularly well catered for in Plymouth and its surrounding areas: **Dartmoor National Park** is one of the finest unspoilt landscapes in the UK, and the coastal footpaths offer some beautiful and memorable views. The **Cornish South West Coastal Path**, for example, runs through Mount Edgcumbe Park to the beaches at Kingsand and Cawsand and then on to Whitsand Bay and Downderry further along the Cornish coast.

The city itself should not be overlooked by walkers: the waterfront walkway, for example, offers many opportunities to explore the city's rich history. Following the footsteps of heroes, you will visit famous landmarks such as the **Mayflower Steps**, the monument that commemorates the point where the Pilgrim Fathers set sail for America, and the **Hoe**. You can pick up on clues left by Sherlock Holmes and discover unexpected treasures such as lumps of gold bullion and a 10-tonne rhino. The route is ideal for families: it is easy to follow and suitable for people of all abilities. If you want a leaflet, you will have to pay for it, but the walk itself is free. You can get all the information you need, however, from a local tourist information centre.

There are many other interesting places in Plymouth and its surrounding areas that you can visit for free. **Barbican**

Glassworks, for example, offers regular glass-making exhibitions and is open seven days a week. **Yelverton Paperweight Centre** is home to the Broughton Collection, a permanent exhibition of hundreds of glass paperweights made by glass artists from the renowned studios of Saint Louis, Baccarat, Caithness and Whitefriars, to name but a few.

The **City Museum & Art Gallery**, meanwhile, houses outstanding collections of fine art, porcelain and social and natural history, and is well worth a visit.

If the weather is fine, why not visit some of the delightful gardens in the area? The **Elizabethan Garden** is set out in true Elizabethan style and is open daily all year. The **Sensory Garden**, meanwhile, has been designed especially for the visually impaired, but will enchant everyone, so remember to add it to your itinerary.

Plymouth also hosts many exciting free events, such as the **British Fireworks Championships**, where for two nights each year the skies over Plymouth Hoe are ablaze with glittering fireworks as fireworks companies vie with each other to put on the best displays. Other recent events have included the **Plymouth Maritime Festival**, the **Formula One Powerboat Grand Prix**, the **Radio One Roadshow** and the **Plymouth Air Show**. There are free concerts too.

The huge variety of attractions going on in Plymouth and the rest of the West Country will ensure that there will always be something to suit you, whatever the time of year and whatever the weather. For details contact either your local tourist information centre or the Plymouth tourist information centre (see Useful addresses, page 199).

BIRMINGHAM: A FEAST OF FREE OUTINGS AND ENTERTAINMENT

You can have a wonderful time in the Midlands without spending anything at all, and nowhere is this truer than in Birmingham. This vibrant city is well known for its style, charm and enviable reputation for world-class sporting events, but did you know that it also has more miles of canals than Venice? You don't need a boat to enjoy the towpaths, however, all you need is a pair of comfortable, preferably weatherproof, walking shoes. You can also explore many more miles of canal towpaths in the surrounding areas. For more information, contact the British Waterways Canal Information Centre (see Useful addresses, page 197).

Birmingham also has its fair share of beautiful parks and other outdoor spaces. **Sutton Park** is Birmingham's largest park and has recently been designated a National Nature Reserve by English Nature. In addition to walking you can enjoy a wide variety of other pastimes there, such as jogging, cycling, fishing, horse-riding, canoeing, sailing, kite-flying and orienteering.

Cannon Hill Park is one of the most popular parks in the city. If you are interested in wildlife, you will find much to inspire you by following the walkways and cycle routes alongside the River Rea. **Woodgate Valley Country Park** and **Lickey Hills Country Park** on the outskirts of Birmingham are also worth a visit.

For indoor pursuits, you are spoilt for choice in and around Birmingham. The collections at the **Birmingham Museum and Art Gallery** have been built up over the last two hundred years, and represent every era of history, art, science and nature, from ancient geological exhibits to feats of human enterprise and creativity. Special events also take place, including children's activities during school breaks.

The **Museum of the Jewellery Quarter** should be an essential stop on your itinerary. It was built around the preserved workshops of a renowned jewellery firm called Smith & Pepper. This award-winning museum presents a fascinating insight into the history of the city's jewellery trade over the last two centuries.

If you are interested in transport, **Coventry Transport Museum** houses the largest collection of British road transport in the world. It features over 230 cars and commercial vehicles, as well as 250 cycles and 90 motorcycles.

Soho House Museum is another fascinating place to visit. It was the home of Matthew Boulton, who was noted for the mark he left on industrial development in the city. If you love historic houses, you will certainly enjoy this one, which has been restored to its full eighteenth-century glory.

You should also visit **Aston Hall**. This Grade 1 listed building is one of the most important historic buildings in the Midlands. It was built in the early seventeenth century and was one of the last great homes to be built in the flamboyant Jacobean style. Its period rooms contain fine furniture, textiles, paintings and metalwork from the collections of the **Birmingham Museum and Art Gallery**.

Blakesley Hall is another historic house that should be on your itinerary. It was built in 1590 for a Birmingham businessman called Richard Smallbroke, and is furnished to reflect the lifestyle of a wealthy family of the late Tudor and Stuart periods.

For art lovers, the **Barber Institute of Fine Arts**, situated in one of the city's finest art deco buildings, is a must. Here you will find impressive collections of paintings, drawings, prints and sculptures. You will also find a prized collection of coins, seals and weights from Rome, Byzantium and the Middle East.

There is also a lot to see and do at the **New Art Gallery** in Walsall. It is the home of the distinguished Garman Ryan Collection, which comprises 365 works of art, including three-dimensional works from different cultures and periods around the world. Most notably, the collection also includes important works by European artists such as Van Gogh, Monet, Turner, Renoir and Constable. The gallery also contains other fascinating collections, including topographical works of the borough of Walsall and its inhabitants during different periods.

Sarehole Mill is another good place to visit. It was built in 1765 on the site of Biddles Mill, which dated back to 1540. It is a good example of one of the many water mills that used to exist in

Birmingham. In addition to the mill you will find an interesting group of buildings, including a metal workshop, a granary and a bakehouse, arranged around a cobbled courtyard.

As you would expect from such a major cosmopolitan city, Birmingham is host to a fascinating variety of free events that reflect the cultural diversity of the region. For example, in October each year, there is a month-long celebration of Black history, celebrating the contributions, struggles and achievements of Black people and the expression of their diversity, culture and heritage. Here you can enjoy a wide range of treats from the arts, music and literature.

In November each year, **Millennium Point** is filled with live Indian music, cultural dance, wonderful foods and exciting rides for children to celebrate the Sikh and Hindu festival of **Diwali**.

Millennium Point is also the key place to see the annual **Christmas Lights Switch-On**, which takes place shortly after Diwali and features local celebrities and a wealth of musical entertainment.

If you are in Birmingham any time between mid-November to around 21 December, you will also be able to visit the large and authentic **Frankfurt Christmas market**, where traders from Frankfurt sell candles, ceramics, glasswork, handmade toys, jewellery and traditional Christmas decorations, as well as hot foods and a selection of delicious drinks.

And what better way to finish the year than by celebrating **New Year's Eve** in flamboyant style at Millennium Point, with a veritable feast of live bands, music, fireworks and entertainment.

These are some of the regular free events that go on in Birmingham. There are usually many other one-off events that take place throughout the year, so to find out what's going on before you visit, contact the local tourist information centre (see Useful addresses, page 197).

Manchester is often called the 'beating heart of the North' and it is easy to see why. It has all the facilities, events and culture you would expect from such a vibrant and thriving city.

Take a stroll around this colourful city, and you can spend many hours appreciating its charms. Walk through **Chinatown**, for example, and see its bustling community and the majestic red and gold Imperial Arch built by Peking craftsmen. Then why not visit the **Chinese Arts Centre**? This presents changing contemporary arts exhibitions and a wide range of interesting information on Chinese art and culture. Near to Chinatown you will also find the famous **Gay Village**, with its waterfront restaurants and bars – an ideal place to sit and watch the world go by. Then why not visit the bohemian **Northern Quarter**, with its trendy people and shops, or **Piccadilly Gardens**, with its pavilion, lawns, fountains and sculptures?

Another area not to miss is the historic **Castlefield**, which is considered by many to be the hidden jewel in the city's crown. This area dates back to 200 CE, and to this day still contains evidence of the Roman occupation and well-preserved fortresses.

There are also interesting canal walks in and around Manchester, and a wealth of beautiful public parks, such as the **Castlefield Urban Heritage Park**, which is an open area of waterways, tourist attractions and cafés. The **Daisy Nook Country Park** includes beautiful woodlands, a lake, a canal, the River Medlock and flower-filled meadows. You can also take in free exhibitions and activities for children at the Visitor Centre.

You may want to explore the surrounding countryside: touching Greater Manchester to the east is the wonderful **Peak District National Park**, with its high moorland to the north and limestone caves to the south. Here you will find breathtaking views and beautiful walks. There are also free guided wildlife walks in the **Mersey Valley**.

Manchester has its fair share of museums and galleries, and many of them are free. The **Museum of Science & Industry**, for example, provides a great day out with lots to see and do. This huge museum houses some spectacular displays, including the oldest passenger railway station and railway warehouse in the world. You can see fantastic flying machines and take a ride on a steam train. Other features include the **Power Hall**, the **Air and Space Gallery** – a hands-on science gallery – and the **Fibres, Fabrics and Fashion** display.

Another must is **Manchester Museum**, which houses collections covering many subjects, including Egyptology, zoology and the science of life. Its geology collection includes some amazing fossils and dinosaurs.

On the art side, **Manchester Art Gallery** houses some spectacular works of art, including the much loved Pre-Raphaelite collection. The **Whitworth Art Gallery**, meanwhile, is famous for its collections of British watercolours, textiles and wallpapers, but also contains a notable collection of prints, drawings, sculptures and paintings.

The Cornerhouse is Manchester's centre for international cinema and the visual arts. Its three galleries feature contemporary art, photography and sculpture. You will have to pay if you want to see an independent film at one of its three cinema screens, but you can see the exhibitions for free.

If clothes and fashion are more to your taste, then you should visit the **Gallery of Costume**, which is an elegant Georgian house containing one of the finest costume collections in the country. The costumes date from the 1600s to the present day.

Manchester also has a whole host of interesting buildings you can visit for free. **Manchester Cathedral** has a breathtaking interior, with fabulous medieval carved woodwork and beautiful modern glass. Guided tours are free, and so are the lunchtime concerts held there and the beautifully sung evensong. There is also a visitor centre, which provides interactive facilities. Also, the

Theological Society gives free lectures at the cathedral about six to eight times a year.

Other interesting buildings worth a visit include **John Ryland's Library**, one of the country's finest late-Victorian Gothic buildings. It houses one of the best collections of manuscripts and printed works in Europe. The library has recently been undergoing a programme of major renovation works, so check that it is open before you go there.

The Pankhurst Centre will provide another interesting stop on your itinerary. This is the house where the Pankhurst family lived. The Pankhursts were key players in the Votes for Women movement, and the Women's Social and Political Union was formed here in 1903.

If you have time, don't forget to visit **Heaton Hall and Park** on the outskirts of the city. Heaton Hall is a Grade I listed house and has some stunning period interiors – the Etruscan room is particularly beautiful. The 640-acre park features a walled garden, pets corner, historic tramline and boating lake, so there will be something to interest adults and children alike.

Manchester also stages many spectacular events each year, and recently these have included street light festivals, colourful parades and carnivals, cultural festivals, jazz fests, shows and concerts. For information on all these free events, and more, contact the local tourist information centre (see Useful addresses, page 198).

CARDIFF: A WEALTH OF FREE OUTINGS

The beautiful Welsh countryside around Cardiff is a haven for walkers, and there are many **guided walks** available, most of them free of charge. You can discover some fascinating archae-ological sites, rare plants and flowers and interesting wildlife here. You can also gain an insight into the area's industrial history, see the beautiful coastline with a themed coastline walk, explore history with a medieval mystery tour, or go on a guided search for medicinal plants. Or why not survey the star-studded night skies by taking a walk with the Cardiff Astronomical Society? On some of these walks you can even practise your Welsh while walking. There are walks to suit people of all abilities – many are arranged by Cardiff County Council or one of the many ramblers' clubs in the area. Simply log on to the Glamorgan Walks website (see Useful addresses, page 198), which gives details of these walks and many others.

Wales's finest landscaped garden lies on the outskirts of Cardiff. **Dyffryn Gardens** features superbly landscaped grounds in the style of a 'gentleman's residence', with individual garden 'rooms', a Roman-style temple, and fountains. There is a charge in the summer, but you can get in free during the winter months. This doesn't matter, however, because the garden abounds with endless colour and form all year round.

Cardiff also has its fair share of museums and art galleries. The **National Museum & Gallery of Wales** was declared one of the UK's top 10 museums by *Which?* magazine. It charts the history of Wales from its creation, with a simulated Big Bang and animated Ice Age creatures, to the present day. It also houses the largest collection of impressionist paintings outside Paris. Here you can see Monet's *Blue Lady* and enjoy inspirational displays of Welsh art. There are hands-on activities for children and adults too, all year round.

If you like the thought of travelling in time, visit the **Museum of Welsh Life** on the outskirts of the city. This spans 100 acres, and is one of Europe's largest open-air museums. Here you can step back in time to experience life in an ancient Celtic village, see life in a 19th-century Welsh farmyard complete with animals, or witness the austerity of a Victorian schoolroom. You can watch time pass in miners' cottages and visit a traditional Welsh grocer's shop. And when you've taken in all the displays, there is also a modern children's playground to keep the kids happy.

The **Turner House Art Gallery** in Penarth is also worth a

visit: it has changing exhibitions that feature works from the National Museum's immense collections.

If you are interested in finding out more about the Welsh government, the **National Assembly for Wales** has a Visitor & Education Centre that is a must. It features interactive technology and, like everything else listed here, admission is free.

There are also free events taking place at various intervals throughout the year. The largest of these is the **Cardiff Festival**, which takes place over a six-week period each summer. Festival attractions and shows change each week, but usually include lots of free events and street entertainment. The Festival culminates in a Big Weekend, with free live music and a spectacular fireworks display.

Cardiff Bay is a popular site for free events taking place on land and water each year. **Cardiff Harbour** recently hosted two world-class water events: the **Honda Grand Prix of Wales** and the **Cardiff Formula 3 World Powerboat Grand Prix**. There are canoeing open days and regattas, marathons and races, open-air concerts and shows, craft exhibitions and carnivals.

Other recent events have included archaeology weekends, and a Winter Wonderland where an open-air ice rink was set up for people to use free of charge. There is always a huge range of free events for families, which will delight children of all ages. Your children can have fun at music workshops, for example, or discover the high-tech world of bats. They can help form a shoal of fish, or try their hand at spotting alien species of plants and animals that have been introduced by humans. Events vary from season to season, so to get up-to-date information, contact the Cardiff tourist information centre (see Useful addresses, page 197).

GLASGOW: ENTERTAINMENT FOR FREE

In Gaelic, Glasgow is *Glas-ghu*, which means 'dear green place'. And with more than 70 parks and gardens within the boundaries of the city, Glasgow certainly lives up to its name.

The 361-acre **Pollok Country Park** has magnificent woodland and shrubs, beautiful rhododendrons, magnolias, azaleas and Japanese maples, and a fine herd of Highland cattle.

Victoria Park should be another stop on your itinerary. It boasts a wide range of formal floral displays, carpet bedding and hollies. Here you will find a pond, children's play areas and the renowned Fossil Grove with its tree stumps that are an amazing 300 million years old.

The Botanic Gardens, with their famous range of glass houses, are a major tourist attraction. They are also a centre of education, conservation and research. The main glasshouse contains a fascinating collection of tropical plants, including begonias, orchids and ferns.

Finally, don't forget **Kelvingrove Park**'s 85 acres, which were laid out in 1852. These feature commemorative statues, fountains and a fine herbaceous border.

Glasgow and its surrounding areas are a treat for walkers and cyclists. The **Merchant City Trail** takes you through the dynamic 'Old Town' of Glasgow, which was originally home to Glasgow's 18th-century tobacco lords. And the **Kelvin Walkway** takes you through Kelvingrove Park to the city's leafy west end. It follows the River Kelvin northwest through Kelvindale to Dawsholm Park.

If you prefer a longer route through the countryside, some start from the city itself. For example, the **Clyde Coast Cycle Route** winds through some of Glasgow's beautiful parks and closely follows the old Paisley and Ardrossan Canal before heading out to Greenock, Irvine and Ardrossan. Another route links the city centre to the Falls of Clyde at Lanark via the scenic Clyde Valley.

If you're feeling adventurous, why not try the route from the centre of Glasgow out to **Loch Lomond**, where you can begin your journey in the bustle of city life and end by marvelling over the haunting beauty and tranquillity of this beautiful loch? If you enjoy a really long trek, you can even continue onwards towards

Balquhidder in the heart of the Scottish Highlands, following forest trails, peaceful rural side roads, disused railway tracks and canal towpaths.

These are just a few of the many walks and cycle paths that are accessible to the public. There are many others, which take in beautiful coastal scenes, breathtaking views, ancient monuments, sites of special scientific interest and forest trails, as well as Celtic, medieval and industrial landmarks. The local tourist information centre will be able to give you details of walks and cycle routes for all ages and abilities.

The **RSPB Nature Reserve** at Lochwinnoch will delight nature lovers. It has a superb mixture of open water, woodland and marsh, where you can observe a fascinating variety of interesting wildlife close at hand.

Going back to the city itself, Glasgow has over 20 museums and art galleries, and almost all of them are free. The impressive line-up of museums includes the internationally acclaimed **Burrell Collection**, which contains over 8,000 art objects collected by the Glasgow shipping magnate Sir William Burrell, and Scotland's oldest public museum, the **Hunterian Museum**, which was founded by William Hunter (1728–83), physician to Queen Charlotte. This museum has some fine displays, including coins, dinosaurs, gems and Roman archaeology. The Hunterian Museum has recently been undergoing a programme of renovation works, so you should check that the museum is open before setting out.

The **Art Gallery and Museum** at Kelvingrove is another popular free attraction and has over a million visitors a year. It houses one of the finest civic collections in Britain. Displays include arms and armour, natural history, archaeology and fine art. It has also been undergoing a programme of renovation works recently so, as with all venues, make sure it is open before you go there.

Another gallery not to miss is the cool and contemporary **Gallery of Modern Art**, which houses four floors of today's finest paintings and sculptures, and installations from around the world.

And don't forget to visit the award-winning **Hunterian Art Gallery**. This presents an art collection that includes one of the most important print collections in Scotland, and attracts visitors from around the world (remember to check that it is open before you set off).

Also worth a visit are the refurbished galleries of the **People's Palace**, which bring the story of Glasgow and its people to life, explaining their impact on the world from 1750 to the present day. If you have time, try to visit the **Provand's Lordship**, the oldest house in Glasgow, which dates from 1471. It contains period furniture and features a medieval theme garden in its grounds.

For book-lovers, the **Mitchell Library** will be an essential place to visit. It was founded in 1874 and is Europe's largest public reference library. It contains over 1.5 million volumes and an impressive array of literature on the history and culture of Glasgow and Scotland. Another important place to visit is the **Centre for Contemporary Arts**. This features exhibitions that embrace all contemporary art forms, including visual art, music, film, performance, dance and the spoken word. There is a charge for films and talks, but the exhibitions are free.

Glasgow also has some fine architecture from different periods, especially the Victorian era. You should also take a trip to **St Andrew's in the Square**, which is a beautiful example of a fine 18th-century church. It has been restored recently and is considered to be an architectural gem. In the basement you'll find a warm and intimate café, which hosts regular free events, such as jazz concerts and Scottish folk singing.

Visiting Glasgow and its surrounding areas is always an eventful experience, with live performances, festivals and entertainment all year round. The **annual fireworks display** in November on Glasgow Green is a spectacular event, with fireworks, lasers, DJs, live music and lots of entertainment for all the family. The **Great Scottish Run** – Glasgow's half marathon – is always an exciting event each September, with lots of fun and entertainment, including inflatable activities, sports events, and live music. Another event not to miss in September is **Doors Open Days**, which provides an annual opportunity to see inside some of Scotland's architecturally and historically significant buildings – like the other events listed here, it is free of charge.

Lanark Lanimer Day, meanwhile, provides an enjoyable village carnival experience, with a variety of stalls and lots to see and do. This is where the old Burgh boundaries (dating back to 1140) are checked and the Lanimer Queen is crowned. Paisley also has its own major outdoor free event – **Sma' Shot Day** – which celebrates Paisley's proud weaving traditions. And the **West End Festival** should be at the top of your list for midsummer celebrations, with the magic of the Carnival Parade and free events in the parks.

This feast of free events would not be complete, however, without mentioning one of the most famous events of the year: Glasgow's **Hogmanay (New Year's Eve) celebrations**. Seeing in the New Year in Glasgow is a truly memorable experience. You can start by celebrating with an atmospheric street party and bonfire in Biggar High Street – a traditional pagan event that is as popular as ever – then enjoy the live music and street entertainment that goes on around the city.

These are just a few of the many free events in and around Glasgow. There are many others, especially one-off events, so to keep up to date on what is going on, contact the local tourist information centre (see Useful addresses, page 198).

BELFAST: LOTS OF FREE THINGS TO SEE AND DO

You'll never be short of something to do or see in Belfast, with its atmospheric history and cutting-edge visitor attractions. Whether you prefer interesting architecture, beautiful gardens and open spaces or exciting and colourful entertainment, this city has it all.

Interesting buildings to visit include **Belfast City Hall**, which is one of the finest classical Renaissance buildings in Europe. This Edwardian masterpiece, which dates from 1906, is finished in Portland stone and is the home of Belfast City Council. Guided tours are available, and interesting features include the ornate dome, grand staircase and the priceless mural of Belfast's industrial heritage by John Luke.

Belfast Castle, on the slopes of Cave Hill, is a wonderful place to take in plenty of historical atmosphere and beautiful gardens. And the early French Gothic **Clonard Monastery** is a must, with its rich interior and mosaics, and polished red granite columns resting on white marble bases.

St Anne's Cathedral is another interesting building to visit. This imposing Hiberno-Romanesque building could be called a shrine to persistence: it was partly completed and opened in the 1890s, but wasn't finished until nearly a century later!

Another stop on your itinerary should be **Malone House**, an elegant mansion that commands stunning views over the Lagan Valley Regional Park. It was built in the 1820s, and the last resident was a prominent grain merchant, who presented the house to the City of Belfast in 1946. There is an art gallery upstairs.

Continuing the arts theme, the **Old Museum Arts Centre** is one of Ireland's leading centres for visual and performing arts. It is located in a Grade A listed building of architectural importance, which was built in 1830 and was the first museum in Ireland. Admission to the exhibitions is free.

Another interesting place to visit is the **Bell Gallery**, which has two well-lit galleries that contain a good selection of Irish paintings and sculptures.

If you have plenty of time on your hands, **Ulster Museum and Art Gallery** deserve a full day to do them justice, with their rich displays of archaeology, ethnography, art, history and natural sciences. The museum's award-winning Early Ireland Gallery and the Made in Belfast exhibits are a must, and the art gallery features exhibitions from the museum's collection of contemporary fine and applied art, including Irish, British, European and American art. One display that deserves a particular mention is the recently acquired Saatchi collection of 12 works by young artists, which is already proving to be very popular. And children will love the Treasures of the Spanish Armada, featuring exciting items recovered from the *Girona*, which was shipwrecked off the Giant's Causeway. The Museum is planning a programme of major redevelopment works in the near future so, as always, check that it is open before you go.

Another favourite with children is **Aunt Sandra's Candy Factory**, where you can watch handcrafted sweets – including honeycomb, fudge and novelty lollies – being made, just as they were in the old days. Some recipes are over 100 years old.

Other interesting places to visit include **Belfast Telegraph Newspapers**, where you can see the actual pages of the next edition being made up for the camera, plus plate-making and printing processes of Northern Ireland's evening newspaper, the *Belfast Telegraph*. The **Wastewater Centre** is also worth a visit. Don't let the name put you off. This centre features an interesting 'Clean and Green' exhibition, and its highlights include a tour to a Victorian sewer, science labs, a steam engine pond and wildlife area. The centre is open from Monday to Friday by arrangement only, so you will need to telephone first.

For those of you in search of the great outdoors, you won't have to travel far to find some exciting places. **Sir Thomas and Lady Dixon Park** is one of the world's best rose gardens. This is where the **City of Belfast International Rose Trials** are held, usually between July and September each year. The park also has a Japanese garden and a play area for children.

The **Botanic Gardens** are also worth a visit. These contain the Palm House and the Tropical Ravine, which is a fine example of horticultural Victoriana. The Botanic Gardens also contain a rose garden and herbaceous borders, which were established in 1920.

Grovelands, meanwhile, with its art deco entrance gates, is situated about three miles south of the city centre, and features ornamental gardens and a sunken garden.

Another worthwhile place to visit is **Cave Hill** country park, which offers some fascinating walks where you can take in interesting archaeological and natural features. You can also climb Cave Hill, past the Neolithic cave, for a panoramic view from McArt's Fort. United Irishmen planned rebellion on this hilltop in 1798. There is plenty for children to do too.

Don't forget **Lagan Valley Regional Park**, which stretches from Governor's Bridge in Belfast to the former Union Locks in Lisburn. The park spans 1,700 hectares of countryside and 21 kilometres (13 miles) of river. The **Giant's Ring** is also a must. This prehistoric enclosure, which measures over 200 metres (219 yards) in diameter, has a dolmen (stone table) in the centre and is open from dawn until dusk.

On the entertainment side, a wide variety of events and attractions takes place in and around Belfast throughout the year. The **Cathedral Quarter Arts Festival** is a dynamic fringe festival located in the historic heart of the city. The festival aims to celebrate the best new local talent, and also takes in the most cutting-edge national and international new works. The visual art exhibitions, street theatre, talks and debates are free.

Also worth mentioning is **Belfast Festival at Queen's**. This is a commercial event, and you will have to pay to see the theatre, dance, visual arts, music and comedy productions. However, they sometimes include free events, such

useful tip

Remember to take a packed lunch or picnic with you. This will ensure that you don't get tempted by expensive cafés and restaurants and will help you to keep costs down.

as processions and firework displays. Events change each year, however, so check with them first.

Belfast also has many colourful parades. The **West Belfast Festival**, for example, features a parade and other free events. Other parades include the **St Patrick's Day Parade**, and the **Lord Mayor's Show**, which usually features many colourful floats on a particular theme. For example, recently the theme was CS Lewis's tales of Narnia, and featured fantastic floats entitled 'Aslan the Lion', 'the Dawn Treader' and 'the Ice Castle'.

For a full list of free events in and around the Belfast area, check with the local tourist information centre (see Useful addresses, page 197).

Making the most of your leisure time

There are things to do for free all around the UK. Getting the most out of your leisure time simply means using your imagination and creativity. Wherever you live, there will be plenty to do for free; it just takes a little time to research and plan. And when you've had your fill of organised events, why not try organising some of your own? A game of football in the park, for instance, will delight children and amuse your friends. Or why not hold a quiz night for friends or relatives?

You may also be able to go swimming for free, or at very little cost. The government has recently been bringing in new initiatives to tackle obesity and get people exercising again and, as a result, there are currently opportunities to swim for free at many public swimming pools in the UK. For example, in Birmingham, children under four years old can swim for free, and children between the ages of four and 16 can also swim for free, as long as they live in homes where the council tax is payable to Birmingham, or attend a Birmingham LEA school. Schemes vary between boroughs, however, and some are more generous than others. In some cases pensioners can also swim for free, or at a greatly reduced cost. There may also be concessions for other people on a low income, such as students and the unemployed, so ask for more details at your local swimming pool.

When you have exhausted things in your local area, try casting your net wider. One of the best things about living in the UK is that you are never far from stunning scenery and popular tourist destinations. Beaches, lakes, rivers and exciting cities are usually within reach for most day trips. To cut down on travelling costs, try taking advantage of bus, coach or rail discounts, and time your trips so that they coincide with cheaper fares whenever possible. This could save a lot of money over the long term, especially if you are travelling with a family. Or why not share the cost of a car trip with friends?

Finally, don't overlook the healthiest, most environmentally friendly and cheapest options: travelling on foot or cycling. Walking is a relaxing, stress-free way of seeing the world, and is excellent for burning excess calories. Cycling enables you to cover more ground in a shorter time, and so is ideal for longer trips. It's also good for building stamina and toning those leg muscles! And children love it. If you don't own a bicycle, remember that there is no need to pay full price for one. As mentioned earlier, you can buy one second-hand or pick up a brand-new one for a fraction of the cost at an auction.

To sum up, therefore, all it takes to get the most out of your leisure time is a bit of thought and research. A little time spent here and there, contacting tourist information centres or scouring local newspapers, will save you money and ensure that you never miss out on great things to do. But what if you don't have the time to look into what's going on in your area or to plan your leisure time more effectively? If a lack of time is your problem, the next chapter is definitely for you.

7 TIME IS MONEY

Time is the most precious thing we have, and it is often fleeting and elusive. Each hour we have is so precious, in fact, that people put a monetary value on it. It may seem mercenary or shocking to suggest that we put a price on time in this way, but in reality this is what people do every day.

Time is a commodity that we continually buy and sell throughout our lives. For example, when you apply for a job, you are in fact agreeing to sell part of your time to an employer for a specified sum of money. Do you have a full-time job? If so, you are selling at least 35 hours of your time each week, and your employer is purchasing that time. If you earn, say, £175 for working a 35-hour week, that works out at £5 an hour (£175 ÷ 35 = £5). You could say, therefore, that you have agreed with your employer that one hour of your time is worth £5, and this is what your employer will expect to pay.

Buying and selling time

Time is bought and sold in different ways all over the world. When you buy salad ingredients and vegetables, for example, do you buy them already washed, peeled and chopped for you, or do you choose the ones you will have to prepare yourself? It takes time to wash, peel and chop these foods, and retailers will pass that cost on to you. Try comparing prices and you'll see what I mean.

At some time in our lives we have probably decided to do something for ourselves instead of paying someone else to do it. Whether it's redecorating the home, doing home repairs or simply doing our own washing and ironing, we have all tried to save money by choosing the do-it-yourself route.

When you do the job yourself, you are using some of your own time instead of purchasing someone else's. If you need to redecorate your home, for example, and your own time is priced at £5 an hour whereas a decorator's is priced at £15 an hour, it makes sense to use your own, cheaper time to get the job done. If you are earning £20 an hour, however, it would be a false economy to do the decorating yourself. It would make better financial sense to employ the decorator at £15 an hour and use your own time to earn £20 an hour at work.

What I'm trying to show you here is that time *is* money. And just as you spend your money, you also spend your time. Whether you spend your time working, resting, socialising or pursuing a hobby, each hour that you spend has a monetary value – and other people will pay a price to acquire that hour for themselves.

Putting a value on your time

In one sense, of course, time is priceless, and it may feel unnatural to put a price on it. How can you price an hour spent with someone you cherish, for example? Yet it is a fact of life that we do set aside a portion of our time to sell to other people, and we accept a certain price for it. That price varies according to the individual – someone doing a cleaning job, for example, will charge less per hour than someone who is working as a solicitor. Nevertheless, in each case a price has been set.

So how much is your own time currently worth? The simplest way to calculate this is to use employment rates as a benchmark. If you currently have a job, simply count the hours you work in an average week and divide your weekly wage by them. For example, if you work 15 hours a week, and your weekly wage is £97.50, then £97.50 divided by 15 gives £6.50 an hour (£97.50 ÷ 15 = £6.50). If you don't have a job, just look around at the kind of job that is within your current capabilities, get an idea of the weekly wage and the hours expected, and do the same calculation as above. If you think you could get work as a driver, for instance, working 40 hours a week for £200, then simply divide the 200 by 40 to get the hourly rate. In this case it would work out at £5 an hour.

Although it may feel unnatural to put a price on your time in this way, it makes it easier to look at your time objectively, to see how much of it you are putting to good use, and how much you are not.

When you start increasing your awareness of the monetary value of your time in this way, and have got used to the idea, you may well find yourself asking questions like these:

- How much time – and therefore money – did I waste on that dispute with the next-door neighbour?
- How much money did it cost me searching for that lost bunch of keys?
- How much money did it cost in total to watch television this week?

Now by asking these kinds of questions I'm not suggesting that we should give up all our leisure time and work round the clock – we all need sleep, time to relax and periods of leisure to spend however we choose, whether that means watching television, going for a walk or partying with friends. Yet being more aware of the value of your time will help you avoid wasting it and will encourage you to put it to better use elsewhere. By 'better use' I don't necessarily mean taking on extra work – although you could do that if you wish. What I mean is you could use the extra time more profitably in other ways, such as planning your next trip with your family, finding out about the cheapest offers or taking up a hobby. You could also decide to devote some of your time to doing jobs around the home instead of paying someone else to do them.

Planning your time

When you are in debt, or struggling to pay bills, it becomes especially important to make use of your time in a cost-efficient way in order to stay on top of things. Your time is your greatest asset, the most precious commodity you have. How are you using it? Do you think you waste any of your own time? Can you recall yourself ever saying, 'That was a waste of time'? The next time you find yourself saying that, you should correct yourself and say instead, 'That was a waste of money', because that is exactly what it is.

Many people have no idea where their time goes or exactly how much free time they have. We all know what time we get up in the mornings, how many hours we spend in our job and how many hours' sleep we need each day, but most of us couldn't say with any certainty how many hours a week we spend watching television, shopping, doing housework, socialising or being with loved ones. Even people who watch their money carefully each week often have no idea how they are spending their time.

In order to identify exactly where your time goes, therefore, and to see whether or not you are making the best use of it, you need to draw up a simple timetable. It doesn't have to be elaborate, just a simple sheet of paper showing a typical week. Divide the paper into seven columns, one for each day of the week, and then divide each day into 24 slots. Each slot will represent one hour (see the sample timetable on pages 120–1).

First put in all the things you do on a regular basis. Start with the time you get up and the time you spend getting ready, then work through a typical day. Your day might include, for instance, going to work (don't forget to include travelling time), or taking the children to school, doing housework and getting the weekly shopping. Put in whatever things you do regularly at weekends. Then decide what time you tend to go to bed each night – for some people this will be the same time each night. For others the times will vary. It doesn't have to be exact: just choose a time that seems realistic and put that down. Then block out the time you need for sleep. For some people that may be eight hours; for others it might be more or less. Whatever you decide, keep it realistic and comfortable.

When you have put all the things you do regularly into your timetable, take a separate sheet of paper and make a list of all the other tasks you should be doing on a regular basis but may sometimes miss. These might include catching up on your correspondence; filing bills and other papers; tidying the garden; doing repairs to your home, car or clothes; or whatever else needs doing.

Weed garden
Mow lawn
Feed indoor plants
Clean windows
Clean car
Check tyre pressures, oil and water
Clean bicycle
Answer letters
Check bank statements
Clear desk
Do filing

When you have listed all the outstanding tasks you can remember, transfer them to your timetable. It is important to allow enough time for them. Since they will vary from week to week, you may find it easier to devote two or three hours on a certain day each week to keeping on top of these jobs.

SAMPLE TIMETABLE

HOURS	MONDAY	TUESDAY	WEDNESDAY
00.00am	Sleep	Sleep	Sleep
01.00am	Sleep	Sleep	Sleep
02.00am	Sleep	Sleep	Sleep
03.00am	Sleep	Sleep	Sleep
04.00am	Sleep	Sleep	Sleep
05.00am	Sleep	Sleep	Sleep
06.00am	Sleep	Sleep	Sleep
07.00am	Get up and get ready	Get up and get ready	Get up and get ready
08.00am	Breakfast	Breakfast	Breakfast
09.00am	Take kids to school	Take kids to school	Take kids to school
10.00am	Start work	Start work	Start work
11.00am	Work	Work	Work
12.00pm	Work	Work	Work
1.00pm	Lunch	Lunch	Lunch
2.00pm	Work	Work	Work
3.00pm	Work	Work	Work
4.00pm	Collect kids	Collect kids	Collect kids
5.00pm	Swimming	Housework	Housework
6.00pm	Kids' tea	Kids' tea	Kids' tea
7.00pm	Kids to bed	Kids to bed	Babysitter Yoga class
8.00pm	Dinner	Dinner	Dinner
9.00pm	Television	Television	Television
10.00pm	Television	Television	Television
11.00pm	Go to bed	Go to bed	Go to bed

SAMPLE TIMETABLE

THURSDAY	FRIDAY	SATURDAY	SUNDAY
Sleep	Sleep	Sleep	Sleep
Sleep	Sleep	Sleep	Sleep
Sleep	Sleep	Sleep	Sleep
Sleep	Sleep	Sleep	Sleep
Sleep	Sleep	Sleep	Sleep
Sleep	Sleep	Sleep	Sleep
Sleep	Sleep	Sleep	Sleep
Get up and get ready	Get up and get ready	Sleep	Sleep
Breakfast	Breakfast	Sleep	Sleep
Take kids to school	Take kids to school	Get up and get ready	Get up and get ready
Start work	Start work	Breakfast	Breakfast
Work	Work	Clean home	Day out
Work	Work	Clean home	Day out
Lunch	Lunch	Lunch	Day out
Work	Work	Shopping	Lunch
Work	Work	Shopping	Day out
Collect kids	Collect kids	Shopping	Day out
Odd jobs	Housework	Shopping	Day out
Kids' tea	Kids' tea	Kids' tea	Kids' tea
Kids to bed	Television	Babysitter	Kids to bed
Dinner	Kids to bed	Night out	Television
Television	Dinner	Kids to bed	Television
Television	Television	Night out	Television
Go to bed	Go to bed	Night out	Go to bed

When you have added in time for these tasks, go over your timetable again and look at the results. If you are spending your spare time in enjoyable ways, such as going out with your partner, socialising with friends, playing with the children or pursuing a hobby, and you are happy with it and feel it has not been wasted, then that is fine. However, you may also find that you have been spending more time on less productive activities than you realised.

In some cases your time might have been squandered not by you, but by other people. We are all familiar with the idea of someone using someone else for money. For example, we may say that someone is 'sponging' off someone else. What is less familiar, however, is the idea of someone sponging someone else's time. Time is money, remember, and some people are very good at using other people's time instead of their own. For example, some people have a knack of getting other people to do things for them, things that they are perfectly capable of doing for themselves, such as writing a letter of complaint. Some people refuse to travel anywhere by public transport and expect to be driven everywhere by someone else, even though they are perfectly capable of travelling by themselves. They complain that they can't get around if that person is not there to drive them. Even if these so-called 'immobile' people contribute towards petrol costs (not all of them do), they are still using someone else's time unnecessarily.

Do you do lots of things for other people that they could quite easily do for themselves? Mothers and housewives still tend to suffer from this more than most people. Male partners and older children and relatives who don't help around the home, and expect all the washing, ironing, cleaning and cooking to be done for them, are still common. In fact, a person's time is rarely so underpriced and squandered as that of some mothers and housewives. Times are changing, of course, and some men are starting to take a more active role in helping with children and household chores, but in many cases the changes are still not happening, or are happening far too slowly.

So you need to find out how you are spending your time, how much of your time other people are spending for you, and if some of the time spent is in fact worthwhile or necessary.

KEEPING A DIARY

If you find you still have blank spaces in your timetable and yet can't account for where the time is going, or you have a vague idea of what you might be doing but can't be precise in terms of time, then you will find it helpful to keep a diary (see the sample diary on page 124). You should do this for at least a week or two in order to get a more accurate idea of how you are spending your time. Make sure you pick a typical week or fortnight, or the results won't be realistic.

Draw up your diary in the way shown overleaf, using one page for each day and then dividing each day into 24 hours. If you are doing it for a fortnight, you will need 14 sheets. Take your diary everywhere with you and fill it in as you go. Starting from the moment you wake up at the beginning of the week, note carefully how you spend your time: include everything you do, even if it is something small, such as making or receiving a telephone call. Make sure you put in your diary exactly how long each activity took. The aim of this is to account for every hour of each day, so that by the time the week or fortnight is up, you have a much more accurate idea of where your time is going.

❂

useful tip

If you can keep your diary going for longer than a fortnight, say for a month or longer, you will get an even more accurate idea of exactly how you spend your time.

❂

SAMPLE DIARY

HOURS	MONDAY
00.00am	Sleep.
01.00am	Sleep.
02.00am	Sleep.
03.00am	Sleep.
04.00am	Sleep.
05.00am	Sleep.
06.00am	Sleep.
07.00am	Got up, got ready, and had breakfast.
08.00am	8.30 Left for work: travel time 30 mins.
09.00am	Arrived work. Coffee 10 mins. Reading articles 50 mins.
10.00am	Typing up report 45 mins. Coffee break 15 mins.
11.00am	Typing up report 55 mins. Phone call to boss 5 mins.
12.00pm	Typing up report 1 hour.
1.00pm	Lunchtime: ate lunch 30 mins. Went to bank 30 mins.
2.00pm	Back to work: telesales 50 mins. Photocopying 10 mins.
3.00pm	Phone calls from clients 15 mins. Reading articles 35 mins. Coffee 10 mins.
4.00pm	Typing notes 25 mins. Phone calls to suppliers 35 mins.
5.00pm	Admin and making list of tasks for next day 30 mins. Travel home 30 mins.
6.00pm	Arrived home, had a coffee, read mail, and got dinner on.
7.00pm	Ate dinner and cleared up 45 mins. Watched TV 15 mins.
8.00pm	Watched television.
9.00pm	Watched television.
10.00pm	Went to bed and read until 10.50. Sleep.
11.00pm	Sleep.

At the end of the period you have chosen, look back over the diary and compare it to the earlier timetable you drew up. You may be surprised at the differences. For example, cleaning your home may take twice as long as you thought, or you may have forgotten to add some regular tasks into your schedule. Your diary will help you identify these 'black holes' in your timetable so that you can either allocate the right amount of time for them, adjust them or omit them altogether. When you have identified all the adjustments needed, make the necessary changes to your original timetable so that it is now up to date and accurate. Then give it one more check to make sure there are no other errors.

Making the most of your time

When you have completed your amended timetable, you will have a much more accurate idea of how you are spending your time. Now you can go through it and see how much spare time you have left. You may decide that you have more spare time than you originally thought. If that is the case, you are now in a position to put some of it to good use. You may decide, for instance, to use some of it to improve your financial situation, perhaps by earning extra income, or to find ways of making savings and cutting costs. Alternatively, you could use the time to take up a new hobby, keep fit or catch up with friends or family. However you decide to use it, make sure you plan in some time for yourself. We all need and deserve some time for ourselves, and making sure you keep some of your time for yourself will help you feel more satisfied and in control of your life. Whatever you do with your personal time is up to you: the only condition is that you should use it only for yourself, not for others. Some people use the time simply to relax; others use it to keep fit, curl up with a book or practise meditation. It's also a great opportunity for taking time out to review your life and current situation, and make changes where necessary.

Reclaiming your time

If you find that, having gone through your revised timetable, you have no spare time at all, or that you are having trouble fitting everything in, then you need to take some serious action. Having too much to do, with no time for relaxation, leads to increased stress; over a prolonged period this will eventually have a detrimental effect on your health, quality of life and overall well-being.

caution

While some stress can be motivating, too much stress over long periods overloads the body with stress hormones and depletes it of vital nutrients. This can lead to physical illness.

Start by going through your timetable and highlighting the tasks that other people could easily perform for you. If you are spending too much time looking after other people or doing all the housework yourself, for example, ask other people to give you a hand. Make a rota, if necessary, and allocate household chores to different people. If the people around you sincerely care about you and your well-being, you should find them ready and willing to lend a hand. If you meet with any resistance, however, it will be telling you something loud and clear: people are taking advantage of you! Don't let them. People who treat you like this are telling you that they respect your time less than their own. So be firm and don't let them get away with it.

The same goes for your work. If you are overworked and stressed out on a regular basis, you need to tackle your employer about it, or delegate tasks to others if you are self-employed, before things get out of hand. Make sure you start and finish work on time – if you regularly find that you have to work overtime because there are not enough working hours in your day to fit everything in, you are overworked! You must take steps to change the situation, or else the quality of your life – and possibly your health – will be affected.

You will find it much harder to get your finances into shape if you haven't got the time to spend sorting them out. Remember that time is money, and you need all the time you can find right now.

While you are reorganising your time, this is a good opportunity to tackle all the one-off jobs you have been meaning to do but haven't managed to get around to doing yet. Take a large sheet of paper and make a list. Include everything, even small things such as oiling a squeaky gate or phoning a friend. The simple act of transferring them from your mind to the paper should be a relief because now you can stop trying to remember them all. If the list looks longer than you expected, don't be put off. It will soon get shorter.

1. Query £20 bank charge
2. Send back faulty radio
3. Mend hole in curtain
4. Fix bicycle chain
5. Repair garden gate
6. Phone Sonia
7. Phone David
8. Book theatre tickets
9. De-clutter spare room
10. Decorate hallway
11. Book holiday

When your list is complete, assess each task and decide if doing it is in fact worthwhile or necessary. If you have any doubts about it or believe that it is not really worth doing, then don't waste any further time on it. Simply delete it. Alternatively, if you decide that it does need to be done and that someone else could do it for you, then delegate it to that person. When you have done this, reorganise the remaining tasks in order of priority by giving each one a number. Allocate number 1 to the most urgent job, number 2 to the next urgent, 3 to the next, and so on, until you have worked your way through the list.

Now go back to your timetable. Make sure you have allocated a regular time each week to do these tasks. You don't need to allow a large chunk of time to do them all in one go: simply allocate, say, two hours each week, and do as many of these jobs as you can in that two-hour slot. Work through the tasks in numerical order, starting with the most urgent, and cross them off as you complete them. Whichever tasks are left at the end of the two hours should be carried forward to the next block of two hours the following week. If you have a job that requires a longer period of time, such as redecorating a room, you will need to allow some separate time for this. The main thing to remember is that your two-hour slot should be used to clear up all those small, niggly jobs that have been hanging around for a long time. Make it a habit to spend two hours each week catching up on them and you will start to feel more in control of your time and your life in general.

Time and other people

When people make appointments and then don't turn up, leaving someone else to waste time waiting around for them, they are showing no respect for the value of that person's time. If people do that to you, remember that they are not just wasting your time; they are costing you money too. And people who persuade you to do things they are quite capable of doing themselves are using you as an unpaid assistant. This isn't to suggest that you should never do things to help other people, but that it is better to help those who genuinely can't help themselves

★

useful tip
Helping people in need is a good and satisfying thing to do, but remember that any time you give to others must be kept in proportion so that you can look after your own needs too.

★

rather than doing things for people who are simply too lazy or manipulative to do things for themselves.

In order to have other people respect your time, you must respect it yourself. Give time to others by all means, but protect it from abuse. And always remember to treat other people's time with respect. What we give out in the world tends to come back to us, and treating other people's time as we would treat our own will set the right example.

Saving time

Always think of your time as a precious commodity. Think of it as money and you will find it easier to look after. Keep looking for ways to save time, just as you would search for ways to save money – after a while it will become a habit. Keep a watchful eye on other people too and make sure your time isn't being wasted. Stay vigilant and be firm with anyone who tries to abuse it. Here are a few tips to help you manage your time effectively:

- Get rid of the clutter in your home and office. Remember that time spent looking for lost items is time wasted. If a lot of clutter has accumulated, allocate a block of time each week to clearing it.

- When you open your letters, have a wastepaper basket ready. Throw away any unnecessary items straight away.

- Answer correspondence the day it comes in, to stop it accumulating. If you can't do it that day, make sure you do it as soon as possible afterwards.

- Limit the amount of time you spend on the telephone. Try to make your calls at times when you can keep them short.

- If you use a computer, be strict with the amount of time you spend reading and answering emails. Allocate, say, 15 minutes in the morning and 15 minutes at the end of the day for emails, and stick to it. Ensure you have appropriate spam filters in place, and watch out for colleagues who keep automatically copying you in on long, unnecessary emails. It is good to be kept informed, but it is unhelpful and unproductive to be inundated with unnecessary correspondence.

- Control the amount of time you spend watching television. Don't simply switch it on and watch whatever happens to be on at the time. Instead, choose the programmes you want to watch, then make sure you switch off the television afterwards.

- Don't let people offload tasks on to you that they can do for themselves. If someone asks you to make a telephone call unnecessarily, for example, explain that you haven't got time and suggest that he or she makes the call instead.

- Practise multitasking. In other words, where possible try to do two or more things at the same time. For example, leave something running on a computer or washing in a machine while you oil a hinge or sew on a button. This works best where at least one of the tasks does not need your constant attention or concentration. Identify all those kinds of task in advance, and earmark them for combining with other tasks.

Keeping track of your time

Each of us has a different amount of time to live in this world. None of us knows with any certainty exactly how much time is ours, but whatever we have is extremely valuable. It's important to protect it and make sure we don't waste it or let other people squander it.

Once you start to appreciate the value of your time, making economies with it will become more natural, and you will feel less inclined to squander it. Everything you do will take on a new meaning, because devoting some of your precious time to something will make you feel that the task is worthwhile. You will make deliberate choices about how to spend your time, rather than letting it dissipate and elude you. Keeping control of your time will enable you to make the right choices, whether you decide to give yourself more leisure time, or spend some of your spare time earning or saving more money. In this way, you should not only find yourself better off financially, but also more in control and able to enjoy a much better quality of life.

❶

caution

When multitasking, never choose tasks that could jeopardise your personal safety or the safety of others. For example, jobs that involve using power tools need your full concentration in order to prevent accidents, and should therefore not be combined with any other jobs that are likely to distract you.

❶

8 UNDERSTANDING BORROWING AND LENDING

'Neither a borrower nor a lender be,' said Polonius to Laertes in Shakespeare's *Hamlet*. While this is good advice in some cases, there are also times when it does not hold true. It is important, therefore, to understand when borrowing and lending are sensible, and when they should be avoided.

One of the most important things you need to clarify before you borrow or invest any money is how much interest will be charged or paid.

Getting to grips with interest rates

Being able to borrow money can sometimes bring a sense of relief. If there is no money to pay a large bill, for instance, the ability to borrow the sum needed and pay it back over a period of time can be a great help.

This help comes at a price, however, usually in the form of interest. Interest is the lender's fee for loaning you the money. It is charged as a percentage of the amount borrowed, so the larger the amount borrowed, the more interest you will pay. For those of you who are not confident about using percentages, I have outlined the basics below. You should make it a priority, however, to familiarise yourself with using percentages as soon as possible, because they are an essential tool in the world of finance.

UNDERSTANDING PERCENTAGES

In order to take complete control of your finances, you need to be comfortable working with percentages. Many people have difficulty understanding them, but they are actually very simple to use once you grasp how they work. Basically, 'per cent' means 'per hundred'. For example, if you see written '1%' or '1 per cent', this means 'one per hundred' or 'one in each hundred'. So if you have £100, and 1 per cent of this sum simply means one in each hundred, then in this case 1 per cent is £1. In the same way, 2 per cent of £100 means 'two in each hundred', so 2 per cent in this case is £2.

If you want to work out 2 per cent of £200, then simply remember that 2 per cent means 'two in each hundred'. For each hundred, therefore, you must allow £2, so in this case 2 per cent of £200 is £4. Use this 'per hundred' rule with other numbers and you will quickly see that the higher the percentage, the more money is involved.

When you look at lenders' fees in terms of percentages, you will see that the higher the percentage, the more money you will have to pay. Let's say Lender A charges 7 per cent interest and Lender B charges 17.5 per cent, and you borrow £100 from each of them for a year. The figures will look like this:

Lender A		Lender B	
Sum borrowed:	£100.00	Sum borrowed:	£100.00
Interest @ 7%:	£7.00	Interest @ 17.5%:	£17.50
Total to pay back:	**£107.00**	**Total to pay back:**	**£117.50**

From the figures above, you can see that borrowing £100 from Lender A at 7 per cent will cost you only £7, whereas borrowing the same sum from Lender B at 17.5 per cent will cost you £17.50. The difference between £7 and £17.50 may not sound like much (£10.50), but if you borrow several hundreds of pounds, the figure increases rapidly. For example, let's imagine you want to borrow £900 for a year, using the same lenders as before. Here are the new figures:

Lender A		Lender B	
Sum borrowed:	£900.00	Sum borrowed:	£900.00
Interest @ 7%:	£63.00	Interest @ 17.5%:	£157.50
Total to pay back:	**£963.00**	**Total to pay back:**	**£1057.50**

The interest with Lender A would cost you only £63, whereas Lender B would charge you £157.50 – that's a difference of £94.50. And what if you wanted to borrow £5,000? Here are the figures:

Lender A		Lender B	
Sum borrowed:	£5,000.00	Sum borrowed:	£5,000.00
Interest @ 7%:	£350.00	Interest @ 17.5%:	£875.00
Total to pay back:	**£5,350.00**	**Total to pay back:**	**£5,875.00**

Lender A would charge you £350 to borrow that money for a year, while Lender B would charge a massive £875 – that's £525 more you would have to pay by going to Lender B instead of Lender A.

Check whether the interest rate on your current borrowing is fixed or variable. If it is variable, it will go up or down depending on current market conditions. This means the interest you are now paying may be much higher or lower than what you were paying when you first borrowed the money. Make sure your current interest rate is not excessive.

★

Interest rates are therefore very important when it comes to borrowing money. The higher the interest rate (the percentage), the more you will have to pay. Do you know what interest rate you are currently paying on your borrowing? If you don't, make a point of checking now. Look through the paperwork you were given when you borrowed the money, or telephone the lender and check the interest rate you are being charged. The result may surprise you.

Getting time on your side

The other important thing to watch for when you borrow money is the effect of time. We already know that time is our greatest asset. Time is money, and we shouldn't squander it (see Chapter 7).

When it comes to borrowing money, the same rule applies. However, in this instance if you waste time unnecessarily, it will actually work against you.

To illustrate this, let's go back to our earlier example of borrowing £100. You have seen that borrowing the money at 7 per cent will be cheaper than borrowing it at 17.5 per cent. However, what also needs to be made clear at this point is that the length of time you take to pay back the money will also have a big effect on the amount of interest you pay.

Until now we have looked only at borrowing money for a year.

When you borrow money for a longer period, then the interest really starts to rise. Borrowing £100 from Lender A at 7 per cent 'per annum' means that you will have to pay £7 'per year' – in other words, £7 for each year that you owe the money. If you borrow that £100 for two years from Lender A, it will therefore, cost you £14 in interest, while five years will cost you £35. Lender B will charge you more because of the higher interest rate: £35 for two years and £87.50 for five years. So the longer you take to pay back what you have borrowed, the more it will cost you in interest. Here are the figures set out again:

Lender A	1 year	2 years	5 years
Sum borrowed:	£100.00	£100.00	£100.00
Interest @ 7%:	£7.00	£14.00	£35.00
Total to pay back:	£107.00	£114.00	£135.00
Lender B			
Sum borrowed:	£100.00	£100.00	£100.00
Interest @ 17.5%:	£17.50	£35.00	£87.50
Total to pay back:	£117.50	£135.00	£187.50

In the five-year example shown here, you can see that the amount you will have to pay back to Lender B has nearly doubled, from the original sum of £100 to £187.50. Imagine how much more that interest would be if you had borrowed several hundreds or thousands of pounds.

To save yourself money, therefore, it is always a good idea not only to secure the lowest interest rate for yourself, but also to borrow as little as you can and to pay back the loan as quickly as possible.

The sooner you pay it back, the less interest you will be charged. So if you borrow £100 from Lender A at 7 per cent interest per annum, but pay it back in six months instead of a year, you will save yourself half the interest and pay only £3.50 instead of £7. If you borrow £5,000 from Lender A at 7 per cent interest per annum but pay it back in six months instead of a year, you will pay only £175 in interest instead of £350.

Before deciding to go ahead and pay off a loan more quickly, however, always check with the lender that there are no 'early redemption' penalties or 'tie-ins'. Some lenders charge these penalty fees if you try to pay off your loan early, in order to make up for some of the money they will lose in interest from you. These restrictions will be outlined in the original paperwork that accompanied the loan. If you are in any doubt, check with your lender first. The moral of this story is, of course, that it's always better at the outset to shop around for loans without these penalties.

Understanding loans

Here is a list of things you should know about your loan:

- What is the interest rate?
- What is the term (period of time the loan is being offered for)?
- How much are the repayments, and how often (for example, monthly)?
- Are there any penalties (tie-ins) for early redemption?
- Are there any other fees, such as administration charges?
- Will the interest rate stay the same over the term of the loan?
- Will the repayments stay the same over the term of the loan?
- What are the penalties for late payment?
- Is it a secured loan or an unsecured loan? (With a secured loan, you will have to offer 'security', in other words an asset – an item of value – that the lender can repossess from you if you do not pay

back the loan. The asset can be your home or any other valuable item that the lender confirms is acceptable. With an unsecured loan, you are not required to provide this security.)

○ What does the small print say? Does it conflict in any way with what is being promised verbally, or is there something in the small print that you hadn't been told or do not understand? If so, ask for an explanation.

Borrowing for the right reasons

The best situation to be in financially is to have no debts at all, and plenty of surplus money and assets producing an income for you so that you don't need to work to earn a living. Having said that, even people who do not need to borrow money sometimes still do so, because there are times when borrowing money can help generate a reasonable profit. It all depends on how they use the money they have borrowed.

BORROWING TO GENERATE AN INCOME

If you borrow a sum of money and then use it to generate enough income to cover the loan repayments and interest and have a comfortable surplus left, you will have an extra source of income and could end up better off.

This strategy works even better if someone else is paying off the loan for you while you still receive an income from it. For example, if you take out a mortgage to buy a property and let it out to a tenant, then as long as the rent you are receiving covers the cost of your monthly mortgage repayments and the upkeep of the property – and gives you a comfortable surplus on top – the borrowing could be worthwhile. You will be receiving an extra source of income each month, and someone else (your tenant) will be paying off your

caution

If you remortgage an investment property to release some of your profits, remember to check your tax situation with an accountant first. In some situations you may not be able to claim tax relief on the additional mortgage repayments, or you may incur an unexpected capital gains tax liability when you do eventually sell.

loan for you. In addition, the property's value may rise, giving you a valuable increase in capital. You could sell the property at a later date and make a profit on the property's rise in value, or you could remortgage to release the profit (as long as the rent still covers the mortgage repayments by a comfortable margin) and still keep the property.

Many people make money by borrowing to invest in property in this way, but as with any lucrative investment, it is important to remember that there are risks involved. For example, if interest rates soar, your mortgage repayments will also soar (unless you've fixed them) and you could find that the rent you receive no longer covers the repayments – in this case you would have to pay any shortfall yourself. You may encounter void periods (when the property is empty), during which you will have to make the mortgage repayments yourself; your tenant may fall into arrears with the rent; or you may lose rent through some other unexpected hitch. The value of the property may also fall. These are just some of the potential pitfalls with this type of investment. However, there are ways of minimising these risks, and if you get it right and do your homework thoroughly, borrowing money for property investment can be worthwhile.

BORROWING MONEY TO BUY TANGIBLE ITEMS

If you borrow money to buy a tangible item for yourself that you believe will rise in value, such as a house, and then it does rise in value, the profit you make could outweigh the money you will have paid in purchase fees, interest and repayments over the years. Also, should bad luck strike and you are unable to make the repayments, at least you will have a valuable item – the house – that you could sell in order to pay off the outstanding loan. You may not even have to sell the house – you could use it to generate income by letting out part or all of it instead. In other words, you have something solid and valuable to show for the money you have borrowed – something that can also bring in an income if necessary. This assumes, of course, that the value of the property rises substantially over a period of time. If it falls in value, or even if the value stays the same, you will lose money in purchase fees, interest and repayments, but at least you could probably let out the property to offset some of the cost. However, remember that while you are living in the house and not letting it, the money for mortgage repayments will have to come from your own pocket.

If you borrow money to buy an item that is likely to fall in value, such as a new car, it will not be such a good investment. As soon as you drive the car away from the dealer, its value will depreciate by around 25 per cent, and over the years its value will fall steadily, until in the end it will be virtually worthless. Although you have a solid item – the car – to show for your money, it will not be worth much after a relatively short period of time. Some cars hold their value better than others, of course, such as classic or vintage cars, and it is also possible to turn certain cars into income-generating assets, such as by using prestigious cars to provide a chauffeur service, but these tend to be the exception rather than the rule. So remember that borrowing money for things that depreciate in value over the years, or for items that will not produce an income, is best avoided.

BORROWING MONEY TO PAY FOR INTANGIBLE ITEMS

A new car depreciates in value over time, but until it becomes worthless you may still sell it and recoup part of the original sum you borrowed. You will have lost a large part of your money, but not all of it. However, people who borrow money for intangible items that have no intrinsic monetary value and no hope of generating any form of income are even worse off. The excitement of getting a loan for a fortnight's holiday in the sun, for example, will soon wear off when the holiday is over but the repayments roll on relentlessly for the next few years. In addition, the holiday has cost more because of the added interest that must be paid.

There are one or two exceptions to this, such as when older people decide to borrow money against the value of their home in order to enjoy themselves and take holidays while they still can. Deals vary, but in many of these arrangements interest on the loan accumulates and then the whole amount is paid off when they sell their home or move into a care home. From a property perspective it is not a sound financial move because the interest will build up until it eats away a substantial part or all of the property's value. However, where time has become more valuable than home equity, it sometimes makes sense to release some of the money in the home in the form of a loan, so that older people (or those who are terminally ill) can have enough money to enjoy whatever time they have left. However, this is very much an exception and is not recommended for the majority of people.

BORROWING MONEY TO PAY EXPENSES

If you regularly need to increase your borrowing because you habitually spend more than you have coming in, and you have no valuable assets to show for it, then this is the very worst kind of borrowing. Unless you reduce your expenditure, you will get deeper and deeper into debt. Borrowing more and more money simply increases your outgoings in terms of higher repayments and interest, and therefore turns up the pressure over time. It is just postponing the inevitable, the day of reckoning when all your borrowing catches up with you and there is nowhere to hide.

People who have several debts at the same time sometimes take out a new loan in order to consolidate all their debts into one loan with smaller monthly repayments. While this can make the overall picture seem less overwhelming, it is important to bear in mind that there are still pitfalls; it should be treated as an emergency measure only and should not be used to increase the overall amount of borrowing. One of the attractions of this type of loan is that the monthly repayments are often smaller. However, they are smaller because they are spread out over a longer

caution

Although taking out a loan to consolidate your debts into one manageable monthly repayment can be tempting, it is essential that you consult a qualified financial adviser first. Each person's situation is different, and what may be suitable for someone else may not be right for you. If you do decide to take this route, it is vital that you check the terms of the deal very carefully and make sure that you will genuinely be better off before you go ahead.

period. This will eventually cost more because, as we have seen earlier in this chapter, the longer it takes to pay off the loan, the more interest will have to be paid. If you are considering taking out one of these loans, talk to a qualified independent financial adviser first, or contact one of the specialist organisations mentioned earlier, such as the CCCS or the Citizens Advice Bureau (see pages 193–6).

REASONS FOR BORROWING

1. DEBTS AND EXPENSES

Borrowing money simply to pay off other debts or to pay for day-to-day living expenses.

2. DEPRECIATING ITEM

Borrowing money to buy an item that depreciates in value, such as a car.

3. BREAK-EVEN ITEM

Borrowing money to buy an item that may rise in value a little so that it can be sold later to pay back the loan and interest and break even.

4. PROFIT-GENERATING ITEM

Borrowing money to buy an item that has a very good chance of generating an income or rising substantially in value, such as a home for yourself, so that you have a good chance of making a significant profit after you have paid back the loan and interest.

5. FREE PROFIT ITEM

Borrowing money to buy a profitable asset where someone else is paying off the loan for you, so that you are in fact getting the item for free. An example of this would be buying and letting a flat or house, where the rent the tenant pays covers your loan and interest repayments and other expenses, and possibly gives you an added income and increase in value on top.

The table opposite highlights more clearly some of the different reasons for borrowing money. They are shown in categories from 1 to 5, starting with an example of the worst kind of borrowing (1) and ending with the most sensible kind (5). This is not to suggest that debts at levels 4 and 5 are desirable, however. Although they present some of the more sensible reasons for borrowing money, and indeed can be a useful tool for generating profit, they should still be treated with caution, and you should avoid like the plague any debt that is difficult to afford, no matter what the category.

You can use this table to help you decide into which category your debts fall. You should consider all your borrowing against the categories given, including any loans, credit cards and mortgage arrangements.

Pros and cons of lending

Learning about good and bad borrowing is only half of the story. In order to manage your finances properly, you also need to be able to distinguish between good and bad lending.

To be a lender, all you need to do is lend money to someone else. People and organisations lend money to each other all the time. But when is lending good and when is it bad?

Generally, any loan where the lender ends up losing money is bad lending. If you lend money to a friend who doesn't pay it back, for example, it is a form of bad lending because you have lost money. If, at the time you gave the money, you had agreed that it didn't have to be paid back, that is different – it is a gift, not a loan, and therefore cannot be classed as bad lending. However, if you gave the money with the expectation that it was going to be paid back, it is a loan and should be treated as such.

Good lending practice should ensure that the lender makes money from the transaction. In no circumstances should the lender lose money. When you take out a bank loan, for example, the lender (in this case the bank) will always make sure that it makes money from the deal. It will charge interest for the time you have the money, and if the loan is over a certain amount, it will usually put additional safeguards in place to make sure it can get the money back if you do not keep your promise to repay. For example, the bank may ask you to offer some form of security against the loan, so that if you do not repay the money, the bank can repossess an item of value from you, such as your home, and sell it to recoup the money it has lost.

LENDING TO FRIENDS AND RELATIVES

Suppose you lend £900 to a friend and that friend takes a long time to pay it back, but does so in the end? Let's say you get your £900 back after one year. Is that an example of good lending or bad lending? It is, in fact, bad lending, because you have still lost money. Not only have you lost the use of that money for a year, but you have also lost the chance of earning interest on it. You could have invested that £900 in a bank or building society savings account that pays, say, 4 per cent interest per annum, for instance, and made £36 in interest over that year. In your friend's case, you may have got your £900 back, but you have lost £36 in interest.

So does that mean you shouldn't lend money to friends when they need it? Not necessarily, but how many people do you know who lend money to each other in the way banks do, taking assets as security and charging interest? And more to the point, how many friends, when they borrow money, offer to pay interest or to give any assets as security, or even offer information about their current financial circumstances? My point is that this kind of informal lending needs to be approached with caution, not just because of the risk of losing money but the risk of losing friendships too. It is also worth asking yourself why that person can't go to a bank for a loan. If a bank won't accept the risk, is it an acceptable risk for you?

LENDING TO ORGANISATIONS

As a private individual, you can also lend money to organisations. Many people already do this without realising it. When you invest £1,000 in a bank or building society savings account, for example, you are in fact lending the bank or building society that £1,000, and it will pay you interest for it. The longer you leave the money with the bank, the more interest it will pay.

Again, you should pay special attention to percentages. In this case, however, you should look for the highest percentage possible, because this time the bank is paying you interest, not the other way round.

The difference between how much interest you will earn with one organisation and what you will get somewhere else can be staggering. Sometimes interest rates vary hugely between accounts run by the same organisation. For example, a couple I know very well recently came into an inheritance of £80,000. When the cheque came through, they put it in the same building society savings account they'd had for the last 10 years, trusting that their money was safe there and believing it would grow. I asked them what interest rate they were currently getting from that account, and they didn't know. When they checked with the building society concerned, they found that they were getting 0.01 per cent per annum. In simple terms, this meant that if they had left their money in there for a year, it would have earned them only £8 in interest.

'That doesn't sound like much interest for all that money,' they said, and they were right. It was a terrible rate. So we shopped around for other options. Simply by opening a new but similar account with the *same* building society, they found they could earn 2.5 per cent interest – that worked out at £2,000 a year, a whopping £1,992 more than if they had left it where it was.

Organisations such as building societies often pay a good interest rate on a new savings account when they first introduce it, but later make that account obsolete, reduce the rate of interest on it

useful tip

For clarity, my examples of interest do not allow for compounding.

Compounding means 'interest on the interest'. For example, when your savings earn interest, from then you will earn interest on the interest as well as on the original balance, and your savings will grow faster. However, compounding can also work against you. If you allow interest to mount up on borrowings, you will be charged further interest on the interest.

★

drastically, and then bring in a new savings account with a more acceptable rate of interest. New savers will automatically get the better interest rate by opening a new account, but loyal, long-term savers, who have kept their money in the same account for years, will suddenly lose out because the interest rate has fallen dramatically. The worst thing about this practice is that these loyal savers are often unaware that this has happened because they receive no notification from the building society, and they continue to lose money year in, year out. This is what was happening with the couple who had put their £80,000 into their old building society account. When they first opened the account, it was earning a much better rate of interest, but this account had been phased out for everyone except the existing investors, many of whom would have had no idea that they were now losing out. In this couple's case, when they went to pay in their £80,000, they were not even told at the counter that they would be much better off putting it into a new account. While many staff at banks and building societies will tell you about better rates of interest on new accounts when you go there, this doesn't always happen, so make sure you shop around.

Going back to the couple's case, we continued shopping around. We found that, if they put their £80,000 into an internet savings account, they could get even more interest – 4 per cent per annum – which worked out at £3,200 a year – an enormous £3,192 more than they would have got if they had left it where it was. It made the £8 a year they were getting in their old account look absolutely pitiful.

In the end they decided against the internet route because they weren't comfortable with the idea of banking by computer, but they did agree to switch to a new account with their existing building society so that they could take advantage of the 2.5 per cent interest rate instead of the meagre 0.01 per cent they had been receiving under the old account. So simply by shopping around and switching accounts, they had earned themselves an extra £2,000 a year instead of just £8.

Making your money work harder

✱

useful tip

If you manage your finances on a weekly basis and find yearly figures confusing, a good rule to remember is that £1,000 a year is roughly £20 a week – it's actually slightly less than this (£19.23) but the £20 a week equivalent comes in handy for working out rough calculations quickly. For example, using this rule, a salary of £15,000 a year will work out to roughly £300 a week. Likewise, if you manage to cut your bills by £2,000 a year, you will be saving yourself roughly £40 a week.

✱

It is always a good idea to get your money working as hard as possible for you. Think of each pound you invest as one more worker in your financial team. Make it a habit to shop around for the best deals. You will notice that the amount of interest organisations will pay to borrow your money varies widely, and you may find all the options bewildering at first. So here are a few tips to help you understand the factors that affect interest rates.

○ **Time:** organisations will pay you more interest if you agree to let them use your money for a longer period. You may agree, for example, to tie up your money with them for two years, and they will pay you a higher rate of interest if you agree not to touch the money during this period.

○ **Risk:** if you agree to accept a level of risk with your money, organisations will pay you a higher rate of interest. For example, put the money into an account that lets a bank or building society invest it on the stock market, and in return for the higher risk you have the prospect of a higher return. You may get more money if the stock market performs well, but you may also lose money if the market falls. The higher the level of risk, the more interest organisations are likely to offer in order to make the deal tempting to investors. It is important to be aware of the potential risks, however, and not to risk money that you cannot afford to lose.

○ **Saving the borrower money:** if you agree to invest your money via a postal account or an internet account, you will usually be paid a higher rate of interest. This is because the organisation that is borrowing your money will be making savings on reduced branch-running costs, so will be able to pass some of these savings on to you in the form of higher interest.

These are just a few reasons why some investments offer better interest rates than others. It is outside the scope of this book to offer specific suggestions as to where you should invest your money, however. Each person's situation and needs are different, so when in doubt you should always consult a qualified independent financial adviser who will do a thorough check on your individual situation and needs and recommend products that suit your circumstances. Remember, however, to check the adviser's credentials and ask for details of his or her qualifications. Ask if the adviser is authorised by the Financial Services Authority (FSA). The FSA is a powerful statutory regulator that provides valuable protection to the consumer. Its powers are wide-ranging and include the authority to impose penalties for various offences and bring disciplinary proceedings and criminal prosecutions where appropriate. It can also demand compensation for consumers.

You should also ask how your financial adviser is going to be paid. Some advisers will charge you in full for their services. Other advisers will charge you nothing at all or only part of their fee, but will instead receive commission or an introduction fee from the company whose products they are selling. If this is the case, you need to know so that you can decide if the adviser's advice is being influenced by this. There are many good and reliable financial advisers out there, and simply getting commission from a company doesn't necessarily mean your adviser is giving you wrong advice. However, if you feel that your adviser is not giving you objective advice, or is steering you towards a certain product without fully taking into account your circumstances, then you may be better off with a different adviser. The financial services industry is taking steps to stamp out the practice of financial advisers selling products that may be unsuitable for the customer merely to earn better commission for themselves, so if you are in any doubt at all, contact the FSA for advice (see Useful addresses, page 192).

Finally, you should be aware that some financial advisers are tied

caution

Some people fall into the trap of thinking that they can take out a loan, invest it in a savings account, and that the interest they earn on the savings will offset the interest they pay on the loan. This is not the case. Interest earned on savings is always lower than interest paid on loans, so the best advice in this case is to avoid borrowing in the first place.

to a particular company – this means they will only be able to offer you products from the company they represent, and not products from other companies that may represent a better deal. Your adviser should tell you if this is the case, and what level of advice he or she is able to give you. If you are in any doubt, always check: you should be clear about whether your adviser is independent or tied to a particular organisation, and what level of advice you can expect from him or her, so that you can be sure you are getting to know about all the best deals on the market.

Forming an action plan

Having explored interest rates and the differences between sensible and bad borrowing and lending, now is the time to go through your outstanding debts and check the rates of interest you are paying. Aim to get rid of the high-interest loans first – these are the ones that will cost you more money the longer you have them around.

Here are some tips for staying on top when it comes to borrowing and investing:

O Keep your borrowing to an absolute minimum and always pay it back as quickly as possible in order to save on costs.

O Whether you are borrowing or lending, make it a habit to shop around for the best deal, and never simply accept the first deal that comes along.

O When you borrow money, look for the lowest interest rate so that you pay back less.

O When you lend/invest money, look for the highest interest rate to help you earn more.

Putting these methods into action will help you lay solid foundations for making the best financial decisions and ensure that you always have an edge in the world of money.

9 MANAGING YOUR MONEY

The aim of this book is to help you get out of debt, not help you get into it. However, it is important to understand how different debts work, so that you can manage them effectively. This chapter therefore explains all about credit cards, mortgages and loans, and how you can ensure that, while you've got them, you can keep them under control and never pay more than is necessary. You will also learn how to manage any spare cash and do regular financial health checks.

Nowadays it has become a lot easier for most people to borrow money, and the huge range of products available can be bewildering. Knowing the basics, therefore, can help you manage your debts effectively.

Using credit cards

If you find it difficult to control your spending on credit cards, then you should avoid them at all costs. If you already have an uncomfortably large debt on a credit card, cut up the card and send it back to the issuer. However, if you are confident that you can keep your spending down, then a credit card can be a useful source of cheap borrowing while you are knocking your finances into shape – as long as it is used sensibly.

The credit card market has become fiercely competitive in recent years, with companies offering all kinds of incentives to secure your business. The shrewd consumer can use these incentives to keep down the cost of borrowing, and in some cases remove the cost altogether for a limited period. For example, some credit card issuers offer an introductory rate to new customers to tempt them to join. These rates may be as low as 3.9 per cent or 1.9 per cent for a limited period – often six months – on new purchases; they may even be 0 per cent in some cases. This means you can borrow money for six months at little or no extra cost whatsoever. This is one of the cheapest ways of borrowing money for short periods of time. Some credit card issuers also give introductory offers on balance transfers, which means you can transfer a debt from an existing card to a new card and pay little or no interest on it throughout the introductory period. However, remember that when the introductory period ends, the interest rate will shoot up, often to as much as 17.9 per cent per annum or higher, depending on the card involved. You should also watch out for 'balance transfer fees' – check to see if the new credit card issuer will charge you before you transfer any outstanding balances from other cards.

CREDIT CARD INTEREST RATE CHANGE

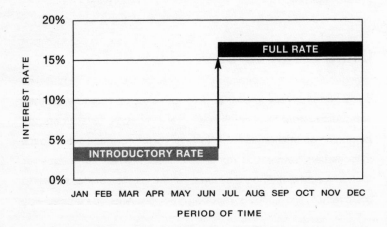

Introductory rates can be very useful temporary measures for cutting down on your borrowing costs. If you have, for example, a £2,000 debt on an existing credit card with a 14.9 per cent interest rate, and a new credit card issuer offers you a six-month 0 per cent interest rate on balance transfers, then it would be worth your while transferring your £2,000 debt to the new card, at least for the first six months, in order to keep down the interest. However, you need to be sure that having a second card will not tempt you to increase your spending, or this will cancel out any savings you will make. Any money you save should be put towards paying off your overall debt balance so that you can see the amount you owe disappear more quickly.

caution

If you are in any doubt about your ability to manage your credit cards sensibly, you should avoid using them and restrict yourself to paying in cash for your purchases.

You will also need to check the rate the new credit card issuer will be charging after the introductory period to ensure that you do not lose money later. If you find that the rate after the introductory period is higher than that charged by your old card, you should transfer the balance back to your old card before the introductory rate period ends to avoid paying interest on the new card at the much higher rate. Alternatively, you could transfer the balance to a new card offering a low or 0 per cent introductory rate, and keep doing this every time an introductory-rate period ends. People who do this regularly are known as 'rate tarts'. It can be a very effective way of borrowing money at zero or little cost, but lenders are beginning to catch on to it so check there are no excessive balance transfer fees before you go ahead. It may work out cheaper to switch to a card offering a permanent low interest rate for the life of the balance. Most importantly, however, you need to be absolutely

✪

useful tip

Do not confuse debit cards or Switch cards with credit cards. If you pay by debit card or Switch card, the money will be taken out of your bank account immediately, and the transaction will not be allowed if you do not have enough money in your account. Credit cards, on the other hand, allow you to borrow the money and pay it back later.

✪

sure that having more cards will not tempt you to increase your borrowing. If you doubt your ability to resist such temptation, leave this method well alone! Remember that rates vary widely between card issuers, both during and after introductory periods, and should be checked carefully. In some cases credit card issuers also charge an 'annual fee', so check the terms carefully before going ahead.

Some credit card companies offer 'money-back' cards. These allow you to earn money every time you make a purchase, usually from 0.5 per cent to 2 per cent of the transaction's value. For example, if you buy a coat for £100 using a money-back credit card that pays 1 per cent on all purchases, you would earn £1 back on that coat. If you paid for a £750 holiday using that card, you would earn £7.50. The card issuer usually saves up these amounts and pays them to you in a lump sum once a year. Some card issuers send you a cheque, while others credit your account balance with the amount you have earned over the previous year. If you regularly pay for things like petrol and food on your credit card, these money-back items can mount up quickly, and you could receive a tidy sum from your card issuer once a year. However, in order to reap the full benefits of this arrangement, you MUST pay off your card balance in full each month, otherwise the interest you pay on your loan will far outweigh any money you get back at the end of the year. If you doubt your ability to control your spending or pay off the balance in full each month, then a money-back card is not for you.

Understanding mortgages

When dealing with mortgages, you should always consult at least one independent financial adviser, but preferably several. The mortgage market is very competitive and there are so many different deals available nowadays that the choices can be bewildering. An independent financial adviser will be able to tell you whether you are currently paying too much for your mortgage and whether you can save money by switching to a different lender.

Basically, mortgages tend to fall into one of two categories: 'repayment' or 'interest-only'. With a repayment mortgage, your monthly repayments pay off two different things: one portion pays for the interest that has accrued over that month, and what is left

REPAYMENT MORTGAGE
CAPITAL REDUCTION

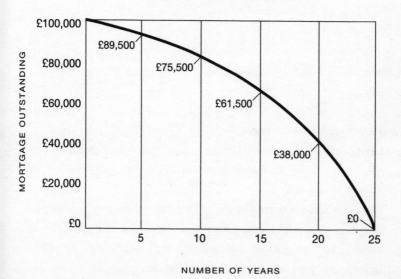

goes towards paying off the sum you originally borrowed (known as the 'capital'). In the early years of your mortgage, a large part of your monthly repayments will be used up paying off the interest, but as you pay off more and more of the capital, the interest part reduces and more of your monthly repayments will go towards paying off the capital. What this means in effect is that, with a repayment mortgage, you can be sure that your loan will be completely paid off when the mortgage term ends.

With an interest-only mortgage, your monthly repayments are used solely to pay off the interest that accrues each month, and nothing is used to pay off the original sum borrowed. This means that repayments are lower, but it also means that at the end of the term, you will still owe the full amount you originally borrowed.

INTEREST-ONLY MORTGAGE
CAPITAL OUTSTANDING

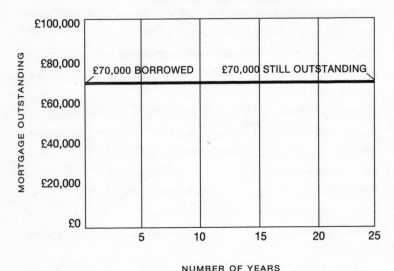

There are various ways of paying off your interest-only mortgage. One way is to make a separate investment that will pay off the outstanding balance at the end of the term. Until recently, endowment policies were popular for this purpose. With an endowment policy, you make monthly payments into a plan: some of it is used to insure your life for a particular sum (usually the amount of the mortgage), and the rest is invested, with the intention of the investment growing enough to pay off the mortgage at the end of the term. However, with falling interest rates and poor performances in the stock markets over recent years, the value of many endowment policies has fallen and many people have found themselves having to make up a shortfall at the end of the term. For this reason, many people have turned away from endowments and have sought other ways of paying off their loans. It is therefore essential that you seek qualified independent financial advice if you have an endowment or interest-only mortgage.

MORTGAGE INTEREST RATES

Different mortgages have different ways of charging interest. If your mortgage is on a standard variable rate, for example, the interest rate will fluctuate according to the bank base rate and current market conditions. If your mortgage is on a fixed rate, the interest rate will be fixed for a set period.

The bank base rate is set by the Bank of England Monetary Policy Committee (MPC). Each month the MPC meets to decide what the new rate should be. Committee members assess the current economic conditions and look at many different factors before deciding whether to leave the bank base rate as it is, or to increase or lower it. In general, mortgage interest rates tend to follow whatever happens to the bank base rate, so it is worth watching this rate carefully.

A fixed-rate mortgage can give you the peace of mind of always knowing how much your monthly repayments are going to be, but they usually come with a tie-in (known as an 'early redemption penalty'). This means that if you pay off part or all of your mortgage earlier than the term of the fixed rate or whatever period the lender originally specified, you may have to pay a penalty, which can sometimes be as much as the sum of six monthly repayments. So always check what penalties may be charged for early redemption.

With a standard variable rate mortgage, the monthly repayments may go up or down from time to time, but generally you have no tie-ins and are free to move around without penalties if necessary.

It is possible to have a mortgage where the interest rate is fixed for a short introductory period – for example one, two or three years – and then reverts to a standard variable rate. If you have one of these mortgages, make sure that any early redemption penalties (tie-ins) end when the fixed rate ends. With some mortgage deals the tie-in period is longer than the period of the fixed rate, and if you try to switch lenders or pay off part or all of your mortgage during this time you could still face a hefty penalty. So always check the length of any tie-in period on your mortgage.

There are other kinds of deals available, such as a 'capped rate' mortgage, where your monthly repayments will go down if interest rates fall, but will not go above a pre-agreed ceiling limit should interest rates rise. This allows you to take full advantage of any reductions in interest rates, while ensuring that your monthly repayments never rise above a certain level.

Do you know how much interest you are currently paying on your mortgage, and whether you are on a fixed rate or a variable rate? If you don't, then you should go through your documentation or make a quick call to your lender to find out. When you have this information, compare your mortgage with other mortgage deals. The quickest way to do this is to log on to one of the many mortgage comparison websites currently available. Simply type the words 'mortgage comparison uk' into any search engine – for example, Google – and you should find a whole host of useful sites that will do the donkey work for you. At a glance you will be able to see which mortgage lenders are currently offering the cheapest rates, along with any fees charged and if there are any tie-ins. If you find a mortgage deal you like on the internet, remember that not all websites are updated regularly, so be sure to check that the information is up to date.

If you find that you are paying more than you need to on your mortgage, and that other lenders are offering better deals, you may be able to save yourself a substantial amount of money by switching your mortgage to a different lender. Remember to check whether your existing mortgage has any tie-ins, however, and if so, how much extra you will have to pay to get out of your current deal. You will then be able to decide whether switching your mortgage is worthwhile. It is also a good idea to contact your existing lender and say that you are thinking of remortgaging with a different lender in order to take advantage of a more competitive interest rate. There is no need to feel anxious about telling your lender that you are thinking of switching your mortgage: people do this all the time and lenders understand that it makes financial sense for you to shop around in this way. Your lender may respond by reducing the interest rate on your current mortgage in order to keep your business. Even if your existing lender does offer to reduce your interest rate, however, don't make your decision straight away. Remember to consult an independent financial adviser because he

!

caution

Your mortgage will be secured on a valuable asset, usually your property. This means that if you fail to keep up repayments, you could lose your home. You should therefore consider taking out insurance to cover your mortgage repayments in case of unexpected events such as redundancy or illness. Your financial adviser will be able to advise you on the best way of insuring against these and other risks. Make sure that you choose a policy that covers all your needs, and check for any exclusions.

!

or she may be able to come up with an even cheaper deal or an arrangement that is better suited to your current financial circumstances.

Understanding personal loans

As I said earlier, the aim of this book is to help you get out of debt, not help you get into it. However, there may be special circumstances that justify looking for a loan. For example, you may be paying too much interest on your current loan, and want to replace it with a loan that charges less interest so that you can pay it off more quickly. What follows, therefore, is information to help you find the right loan, but remember: you should borrow only what you absolutely need, and you should be aiming to reduce your overall borrowing, not increasing it.

The personal loan market is fiercely competitive nowadays, and many new lenders have appeared on the scene – even supermarket chains are offering loans these days. So shop around for the best deal, and do your research as thoroughly as possible. Deals vary widely, and you could well save yourself hundreds, or even thousands, of pounds by securing the very best terms for yourself.

Don't assume, however, that your own bank or the bank nearest your home or place of work will offer the most competitive deal – it often pays to widen your search. Many internet banks, for example, offer loans at much lower rates of interest than those offered by traditional banks. There are also other lenders offering competitive deals, so allow yourself enough time for research.

When you find a deal that looks reasonable, check the small print and find out whether the loan is secured or unsecured. If it is a secured loan, the lender will require you to put up a valuable asset to cover the loan should you default on payment. The asset may well be your home, which you could lose if you do not keep up repayments. With an unsecured loan, you will not have to offer an asset as security.

Make sure you check all the terms of the loan, and whether the repayments will be fixed for the length of the term or whether they will fluctuate. In order to organise your personal finances properly, you need to know exactly what you will have to pay over the term of the loan, so getting the right information is vital. To help you with this, refer back to the section entitled 'Understanding loans' on page 138, which lists the things you should remember to ask about your loan.

It is also worth bearing in mind that personal loans usually have higher rates of interest than mortgages, and have to be repaid over a shorter period of time. As a result, you may well find that the monthly repayments on your loan are higher than they would be if you borrowed the same amount on a mortgage. This is mainly because the loan has to be repaid in a shorter time than a mortgage, but it is also due to the higher interest rate charged. You may therefore find it easier to remortgage your home in order to give you a lower interest rate and smaller monthly repayments. However, remember that choosing the mortgage route will mean the loan will take much longer to pay off, and as a result you will ultimately pay more in interest, even with the lower interest rate. Each person's situation is different, so once again the best course of action is to consult an independent financial adviser, who will be able to give you specific information relating to your circumstances, and help you make the right decisions.

As with any borrowing, remember one simple rule: never borrow more than you really need – keep your borrowing down and you will ultimately have more money in your pocket. One of the best ways of improving your financial situation is always to keep a close eye on your borrowing. Keep reviewing your borrowing arrangements and see if you can get better deals elsewhere. A few phone calls may be all you need to save yourself a substantial sum, and to ensure that your monthly repayments stay within limits that you find easy to manage.

Making your money work for you

Until now we have been focusing on getting the cheapest deals for your borrowing, but what about if you have any spare cash? The first thing to remember is that your cash will earn a lot less for you in a savings account than if you use it to pay off some of your borrowing. This is because you will be paying a much higher interest rate on your borrowing than you will be receiving on your savings. However, it is always wise to keep some cash handy for emergencies – experts recommend that you should keep at least three months' worth of your salary in an instant access savings account, just in case. While you have a debt situation this will probably not be possible, and you should make paying off your debts a priority, especially if you are paying a high rate of interest on them. Eventually, however, when you have knocked your finances into shape, your next aim should be to set aside some cash to cover any emergencies.

When you do have some spare cash, you should always shop around for the best place to put it. In Chapter 8 we looked at how savings accounts vary widely in the amount of interest they pay (see pages 147–9), and what you can do to earn a higher rate of interest. Make sure you earn the highest possible interest for your money by researching the market carefully and finding the very best deals.

At the very least, you should make sure that your money is earning more than the current rate of inflation. If the rate of inflation is, say, 2.5 per cent, you should make sure your money is at least earning this amount net (after tax) each year, otherwise inflation will be eating into your nest egg and you will, in effect, be losing money. This is why experts urge you not to store your money under your bed – apart from the obvious security risk, your money will gradually disappear through the effects of inflation.

It is not within the scope of this book to suggest particular investments. Market conditions are always changing, and the best investments today are not necessarily the best investments tomorrow.

Stocks and shares, for example, have traditionally been regarded as the best performing investments over the last few decades, but recent falls in stock-market returns have driven investors into other forms of investment, such as property. The best course of action, as always, is to do your own research, and consult an independent financial adviser who will be able to suggest an investment strategy to suit your personal needs.

Reducing your tax liability

To achieve real financial independence, you will also need to take taxes into account when planning your finances. The world of tax is very complicated and can be overwhelming for the uninitiated, but it is important to get to grips with the basics in order to know how different taxes can affect you. Getting the right tax advice will help you avoid any large unexpected tax bills, such as when you sell a house or some shares, or give money to loved ones. Yes, even giving money away can trigger a tax bill in certain situations!

A suitably qualified tax adviser can also help you find out if you are entitled to any tax rebates, and help you claim back the money. As explained earlier (see page 42), HM Revenue & Customs publishes all kinds of leaflets to help guide you through the maze of taxes and tax credits, but unless your financial situation is extremely basic, the quickest and easiest way of dealing with this is to consult a qualified accountant. You may well find that the money the accountant saves you more than covers his or her fee. Even if you don't save any money (which is unlikely), you will have saved a lot of your own time, which as we discussed earlier (see pages 115–8) has a monetary value in its own right. And the peace of mind you will gain from knowing that your tax affairs have been sorted out by an expert is priceless. Even if you have a fairly good working knowledge of basic tax rules, remember that tax rules and allowances change frequently, and it is the accountant's job to keep up to date with these changes. Many accountants also offer a free initial consultation in which you can discuss your situation and get details of fees for any future work.

Keeping your finances healthy

The best way to keep your finances in the peak of health is to do a financial health check every six months while you are clearing your debts, and then at least once a year thereafter. Try linking it to a memorable date that you won't forget, such as a birthday. Check any borrowings, including your mortgage, and see if their interest rates have risen or fallen. Do they still represent the best value for money? Look at what is currently on offer elsewhere, and see if you can get a better deal. Then do the same for any savings or investments.

Cutting down on your expenditure should become a regular habit. It is amazing how expenses can creep up again when you take your eyes off them. As part of your financial health check, go through all your regular bills, and see if any of them can be reduced. For example, new mobile phone deals come out all the time. Your current mobile phone arrangement may have been the best deal six or twelve months ago, but is that still the case? The same applies to all your other regular expenses, from electricity and gas to motor and home insurance. To help you identify all the expenses that could be reduced, go through Chapter 4 again (see pages 55–71).

Don't forget to check your income too. Are there any ways you can increase the amount of money you have coming in? Assessing and increasing your income should be an important part of your financial health check. To help you identify potential ways of increasing your income, go through Chapter 3 whenever you need a reminder (see pages 39–53).

If you keep to this plan, and perform regular checks on all

aspects of your finances, you will get out of debt, and will stay in the black forever. Eventually, organisations will be paying *you* handsomely for borrowing *your* money, rather than you having to pay large amounts for borrowing theirs. This is the true road to financial independence, which leads to lasting peace of mind and freedom from money worries.

10 BARGAIN HUNTING AND SHOPPING FOR FREE

Earlier we looked at the importance of keeping your spending to a minimum, but what happens when you do need to buy things? Not simply day-to-day shopping for food but other items, such as a washing machine or a car, or some new clothes? And when it comes to taking a holiday, how do you ensure you get the best possible holiday at the cheapest price?

If you want to be free financially, you should make it a rule never to pay full price for anything. In fact, wherever possible, try to get what you want for free. This is especially important while you are getting out of debt. If there is absolutely no way of getting an item for free, then at least make sure you get it for the cheapest price possible.

Getting things for free can be easier than you think. Chapter 6 looked at how you can get free outings and day trips all around the UK, and in this chapter we will take a look at some of the other things you can get for free, or at least at a huge discount. From holidays in the UK and abroad to a whole host of other treats, such as designer clothes and jewellery, there will be something here to capture your interest. And there is no need to pay over the odds either: from computer equipment, bicycles, furniture and cars to office goods and stationery, everything is covered in this chapter. All you need to do is spend a little time doing some research or shopping around, and you will find huge savings can be made. This chapter will show you exactly what to do, and you'll even find some addresses, telephone numbers and websites at the end of this book to get you started (see Useful addresses, pages 199–205).

Pay little or nothing for holidays

You really can get your holidays for free, or dramatically cut their cost to suit your budget. Here are some of the methods you can use.

ARRANGE GROUP BOOKINGS

If you know you can get a few friends or relatives together for a holiday, why not offer to arrange the whole thing for them and earn a free holiday for yourself in the process? Many travel firms offer discounts for group bookings, and you can use these discounts to get your own holiday for free. Let's say, for example, that there are 10 of you, and you have decided on a fortnight's safari in Kenya. You ask the travel firm for a group booking discount, and the firm offers you 10 per cent off the total price. In other words, you will save the cost of one person's holiday. You could use this discount to get your own holiday for free, in exchange for organising everything on everyone's behalf. People who regularly go on holiday together could take it in turns to organise the group's trip and get their own holiday for free.

Offers vary from one company to another, so shop around for the best prices and discounts. Check how many people you will need to qualify for a particular discount because minimum numbers can vary.

Groups of people can benefit in other ways too. For example, getting a group together to rent a holiday cottage can dramatically cut the cost to each person because the overall rent can be shared between a larger number of people. Remember, however, that this doesn't work with holidays that are priced per person.

DO A HOME EXCHANGE

This method of arranging a holiday is becoming increasingly popular. Basically, you exchange your home with someone else's in an agreed destination for a specified length of time. You stay in their home, and they stay in yours. There are many advantages to this arrangement:

- You are not restricted to booking in weekly 'blocks': the length of your holiday is entirely up to you and your exchange partner.

- The accommodation is free – all you will need to pay is a small fee to an agency for helping you identify the right property and giving you the contact details. For example, one online agency currently charges £21 for a year's membership.

- The accommodation will have a more personal feel because it is someone's home.

- You may be able to exchange other things too, such as your cars.

- The range of accommodation can be huge, from an apartment in New York or a villa with swimming pool in the Caribbean, to a castle in Scotland or a château in France – in fact, anywhere that people have made a home for themselves.

- You can get all sorts of useful information about the neighbourhood from your exchange partner in advance.

○ You can offer your exchange partner other helpful extras, such as arranging for a neighbour to be on hand in case he or she needs quick, practical advice from someone who is familiar with the area.

To get you started, at the back of this book you will find details of home exchange agencies that will help you find your ideal holiday home (see Useful addresses, page 200). You can find more agencies on the internet. Key the words 'home exchange holiday' into any search engine, and a list of agencies will appear at your fingertips. Look for established firms and check their credentials. Shop around until you find the right agency. As an added precaution, ask for references from satisfied customers.

⭐

useful tip

Always inform your insurers before you let someone else use your home or your car. You may find that there are restrictions, or that you have to pay an extra premium to cover any additional risks, but it is better to disclose the arrangement than to have a later claim rejected.

⭐

WORKING HOLIDAYS

If you don't mind earning your keep, there are many ways you can get your holiday travel, board and lodging for free, and in some cases even earn a small income. You can travel around the world, earning your keep as you go.

The internet is a valuable source of information on working holidays. Simply type 'working holidays abroad' into any search engine, and a variety of helpful websites on work abroad will appear instantly. You will find information on a wide range of job opportunities, from skiing jobs in the Alps or camp-leader work in the United States to tourism, catering and teaching jobs. You could teach English, for example, in places such as China, Africa or Latin America.

Whether you want to fill a gap year, live abroad for a period of time or simply have the holiday of a lifetime, working abroad is an economical way of seeing the world. You will also get an insider's view of different countries, rather than simply seeing them from a tourist's perspective.

If you are interested in working abroad, you should check out the books available in bookshops and libraries. You will find a good selection of helpful guides offering practical advice and information on all aspects of working holidays around the world.

caution

Laws vary in different countries, and if you use an employment agency based in a foreign country you may not get adequate consumer protection there, so choose your agency carefully.

Remember, also, to check your insurance position. You may need additional health insurance to cover you in foreign climes. If you have a permanent home in the UK, you will need to negotiate with your home insurer because many home insurance policies become invalid if the property is left unoccupied for longer than one, two or three months.

Consult your doctor about any vaccinations you may need before you go abroad. Some vaccinations are administered over a period of time, so you should allow at least eight weeks before your departure date to get them organised.

You can also take working holidays closer to home. Working holidays are available all around the UK, and are a great way to travel and make friends. For example, you could do hotel and bar work and earn around £180 per week, with free accommodation and food thrown in. The internet is, once again, an excellent source of information here. Simply type the words 'working holidays uk' into any search engine for a host of websites offering useful advice and details of suitable jobs. To get you started, addresses of a couple of websites giving details of working holidays in the UK and abroad have been included at the back of this book (see Useful addresses, pages 200–1). There are many others, however, so shop around and compare what is on offer. Remember to check the credentials of all companies before using their services, and look for recommendations from satisfied customers wherever possible.

If you are interested in conservation work, some charities offer working holidays that help to protect the countryside. The National Trust, for example, offers working holidays at a wide selection of its properties around the UK. You can choose the type of work you would like to do, and learn how to care for the countryside at the same time. The National Trust makes a small charge to help with costs, but it is still a much cheaper way of holidaying in beautiful and inspiring locations, and you will gain valuable conservation work experience at the same time. You can find contact details at the back of the book (see Useful addresses, page 191).

ENJOY LOTS OF LEISURE TIME AS A HOUSE-SITTER

If a working holiday sounds like too much hard work, why not become a house-sitter instead? Many home owners find it reassuring to have someone staying in their home while they are away, to deter burglars and to give the impression that the property is occupied. Duties will vary in different households. Normally you will bring in the mail and make sure that nothing is left piling up conspicuously on the doorstep. You may also be asked to water house plants and take messages from callers, and in some cases perhaps feed and exercise pets. Before applying for a house-sitting job, check the duties you will be required to perform and exactly how much time you will be expected to spend inside the property.

In return you will get free accommodation. Sometimes you will also get a small wage, and perhaps money towards your travel and food costs. House-sitting jobs are available all around the UK and in many parts of the world. House-sitting agencies are also listed on the internet. All you need to do is type the words 'house sitting' into any search engine, and you will find a list of relevant websites. Some agency websites simply feature advertisements that enable home owners and house-sitters to contact each other. Other agencies actually employ house-sitters to work for them. Agencies that employ house-sitters will usually require satisfactory references from applicants.

HOLIDAYS ON A BUDGET

When you have a little more money to spend, you can start casting your net wider, yet still get the very best deals possible. For example, camping holidays are very cheap and can be great fun for adults and children alike. If you have never been camping, or the last time you went was many years ago, you'll find everything has become much easier and more convenient these days. Tents are now very easy to erect, and you can buy them new at very low prices. Alternatively, you could buy one second-hand or even borrow one from a friend.

It is amazing how easy, cheap and comfortable camping can be. Many sites have toilet blocks where you can take hot showers and wash your clothes. For a small extra fee, you may be able to hire an electric 'hook-up' to your tent, so that you can use electrical

Try cutting down on travel costs by sharing a car or petrol costs with other people. Shop and café windows, local newspapers and the internet are all good places for car sharers to advertise. Alternatively, look for special offers from coach and rail operators.

★

appliances such as hairdryers or kettles in the comfort of your tent. Also, if you have a car, you can find all kinds of gadgets that will run from your vehicle's cigarette lighter. For a good night's sleep, an inflatable mattress is essential (a beach lilo could do the job), and you can get away without a sleeping bag by using a duvet instead.

Small, disposable barbecues, which are available from many supermarkets and camping shops, are ideal for cooking quick meals near your tent and save splashing out on expensive meals in cafés or restaurants. On my last camping trip, we used them to cook veggie burgers and sausages in buns in the evenings, and toasted teacakes in the mornings. Many sites run shops where you can purchase essentials such as milk, butter and bread, and they may also let you put your cooler-bag ice-packs in their freezer. Campsite owners are usually very friendly and helpful, and will give you all sorts of useful tips for making your stay as comfortable and enjoyable as possible. And although tents are very easy to erect these days, you can often hire a tent that is already erected and equipped for you if you prefer. Some 'chalet' tents are very luxurious – it all depends on your budget. These usually need to be booked in advance, so check with the site owner first.

Facilities differ greatly between campsites: some sites are small and quiet, and others are large, energetic places with clubhouses, cafés and playgrounds for children. Some sites have indoor or outdoor swimming pools, and some welcome dogs. You can also choose from a wide variety of locations, from woodlands to beach sites. Many campsites are situated in beautiful countryside, popular resorts or places of historic interest.

Camping is a flourishing business: there are many well-equipped and organised campsites all over the UK, and many more abroad. For a few pounds a night, you can enjoy exciting holidays that everyone will remember, whether you are a family looking for lots of activities, entertainment and adventure, or a couple looking for romance and alfresco meals under the stars.

There is an enormous amount of information on the internet, and at the back of this book you will find addresses of some websites to get you started (see Useful addresses, pages 199–200). You can find others by keying the word 'camping' into any search engine. Some websites display colour photos so that you can get a more accurate impression of the sites and their facilities.

If your budget will stretch a little further, you might consider staying in a caravan. These can be amazingly cheap if you go in a group and split the cost between you. Many sited caravans these days have every modern convenience, from separate bedrooms and a comfortable lounge and kitchen to flushing toilets and hot showers. Touring caravans are another option, although the cost of caravan hire, petrol, insurance and parking will push up the budget considerably. If you take the caravan abroad, you will also have to take into account the cost of passage overseas (by ferry or tunnel) and motorway tolls.

If you decide to make camping or caravanning a regular pastime, then joining a camping or caravan club could be useful. In addition to providing lots of helpful advice and information, these clubs often give discounts to members, which could help you recoup your membership fee and keep your holiday costs to a minimum. To get you started, you will find details of one such club at the back of this book (see Useful addresses, page 199). There are others, however, and you should shop around because membership fees and discounts vary. If you have access to the internet, simply key the words 'camping club' into a search engine and you will find many more clubs to try.

CUTTING COSTS OF OTHER HOLIDAYS

As your financial situation improves, and you have more money at your disposal, it is still a good idea to shop around for the best deals. Cutting down on unnecessary costs will give you extra spending money when you are on holiday. Here are a few tips:

- Look for last-minute offers: hotels, airlines and travel firms often give substantial discounts on unsold tickets and last-minute cancellations. Shop around and search the internet for the cheapest deals. At the back of the book you will find details of a website that offers last-minute deals (see Useful addresses, page 201), but check out other websites so that you can compare them. Teletext is another good source of bargain holidays.

- Time your holiday to avoid peak periods: prices of holiday accommodation and travel tend to soar in popular periods. Examples of expensive periods include Easter holidays, Christmas, and New Year and other bank holidays and school holidays. If you are taking a short break, check whether certain days of the week are cheaper than others.

- Always shop around. Even the same holiday package may be cheaper with one firm than with another.

- Check for additional charges, such as airport taxes and supplements for single rooms or sea views.

- Look for special offers, such as one free night in every seven, or children under a certain age travelling for free.

- If you are booking direct with a hotel, try haggling on the price. Hotels need to keep their rooms occupied, and are often willing to reduce their prices in order to fill rooms that are vacant due to cancellations or during less busy periods. You may be able to secure a discount on the cost of your room, or get breakfast thrown in for free.

- Keep an eye on newspaper and magazine advertisements for holiday bargains.

- Ask hotel companies and travel operators to add you to their mailing lists, so that you get to hear about any special offers.

Cutting the cost of your shopping

The habit of never paying full price for anything can work just as well with your shopping as it does with holidays. Next time you need to buy an item, don't simply head for your nearest high street and pay full price for it. Work out in advance exactly what it is you need, and stick to it. Don't be tempted to overspend on more sophisticated versions. After you have decided on your product, aim to reduce the cost substantially by doing your homework, comparing prices and seeking the best discounts you can find. Getting a bargain in this way is very satisfying, and your bank balance will be all the better for it.

The same method works for all kinds of items. For example, when you need to buy clothes, why pay full price when there are lots of bargains to be had? Plan your shopping around seasonal sales – almost every retail outlet has some kind of January sale, and many others hold them at other times of year, such as end-of-summer sales. This helps the retailers clear the previous season's stock, and helps the consumer – you – get the goods for a fraction of the cost.

BARGAINS IN FACTORY SHOPS AND OUTLET VILLAGES

Factory shops, and outlet shops and villages are a good source of bargains and can be found all over the UK. They offer a wide range of heavily discounted goods, including branded and designer clothing for adults and children, household and garden products, electrical goods, hardware, toiletries and cosmetics, books, toys, furniture and soft furnishings, sportswear, footwear, accessories, jewellery and gift items. Discounts can range from anywhere between 25 and 70 per cent off the retail price.

There is a distinct difference between a true factory shop and an outlet shop. True factory shops are often situated on trading estates and behind industrial towns. In these shops you can find new-season styles and colours and sample one-off items, as well as overstocked items and slightly imperfect goods. Outlet shops and villages tend to stock more of last season's items, and can often be found in large shopping centres. Whichever you choose, always check a shop's returns policy, and make sure that any electrical goods come with a guarantee. Check for flaws and defects in the goods before buying them. If you do buy an item and later discover a defect, however, there is no need to worry. You have the same statutory rights in these shops as you would in any UK shop, so you can make your purchases with confidence.

To find factory or outlet shops in your area, type the words 'factory shops uk' into any internet search engine. You will also find contact details of a few shops at the back of

useful tip

Find out the retail price of any products in which you are interested before you go to a factory shop or outlet. Knowing the high-street price will help you decide if the discount price you are being offered by a factory shop or outlet represents a true bargain.

the book (see Useful addresses, pages 202–3) to get you started. Always telephone before you go to make sure that the shop will be open and that it stocks the kind of products you need.

CATALOGUE SURPLUS SHOPS

These are another useful source of bargains, where you will find surplus stock being sold at prices significantly lower than normal catalogue prices. Products range from clothes and shoes to toys, household products and electrical goods. You will find some contact details in Useful addresses, page 203. Alternatively, type the words 'catalogue surplus' into any internet search engine, and a list of shops will appear.

WHOLESALERS AND CASH-AND-CARRY SHOPS

If you run a business, you should look into the substantial savings you can make at cash-and-carry shops and wholesalers. You can buy all kinds of goods at cut prices here, from clothing and household products to food and drink, office goods and stationery. Two of the best-known cash-and-carry chains are Booker and Makro (see Useful addresses, pages 201 and 205). You could cut the cost of your office supplies, for instance, or substantially reduce your food and drink bills. Many cash-and-carry shops require proof that you are a trading business, so check what you will need to produce before you visit.

BUYING AT AUCTION

You can buy goods at amazing prices from auctions, whether you bid in person at auction rooms or bid online using an auction website. You can find an enormous range of items here, some at a fraction of what you would be expected to pay on the high street. From jewellery and computer equipment to furniture, bicycles, cars and holidays – even homes can be purchased at auction. Sometimes lots are sold with no reserve prices, which means you could end up paying a fraction of their worth. For example, you could pick up a gold diamond ring worth £1,000 for £100 or less, or a personal computer worth £850 for £50. It all depends on how many bidders there are and the price they are prepared to pay. If you are lucky enough to be the only bidder, you could end up with an amazing bargain. If there are other bidders equally determined to have the item, however, you will have to decide how far you are prepared to bid against them. Always check the high-street price before deciding what price would represent a bargain to you, and don't go over your chosen limit.

It is a good idea to watch a few auctions in progress before you start bidding, so that you can familiarise yourself with the process. Also, check the auctioneer's terms and conditions, and any fees payable, before bidding. At the back of the book you will find contact details of some auction rooms and websites (see Useful addresses, pages 203–5). There are many more of them, however, which you can find by keying the word 'auction' into any internet search engine.

USING AN ALTERNATIVE MONEY SCHEME

Does your neighbourhood operate an alternative money scheme? Basically, it works very much like a barter system. Barter is often looked upon as an old-fashioned means of exchange, but it is currently experiencing a revival. To give you an idea of how it works, let's take a look at the system that operates in Cambridge.

Cambridge has its own alternative currency, known locally as 'cams'. Whenever you perform a service for someone, you earn cams. Likewise, when someone performs a service for you, you pay for it in cams. So you could, for example, do some decorating for someone and get paid in cams, and then use those cams to pay someone else to do some plumbing work for you. In other words, you get things done for yourself by doing things for others. Transactions are not taxable because they are classed as an 'occasional social favour' and not regular trading. If you would like to check out the Cambridge system in more detail, the website details can be found in Useful addresses, page 202.

Many towns and cities in the UK operate a system like this. For example, Manchester's currency is the 'bobbin', while Totnes uses the 'acorn'. In St Neots they use 'saints', and in Brighton they use 'brights'. There may well be a system like this in your own area. If not, you could set one up yourself. Some of these systems are listed on the internet under LETS (Local Exchange and Trading System). Unfortunately, simply typing 'LETS' into a search engine can bring up all kinds of accommodation agency websites too, so try refining your search by adding words such as 'currency' and 'barter'. Fortunately, there is also a website that provides links to many of the LETS systems around the country. It is called LETSLINK UK, and you can find the details in Useful addresses, page 204. You could also try making enquiries at your local town hall or community centre to see if such a system operates in your neighbourhood.

Joining one of these schemes can be a very good way of getting what you need without having to pay cash for it – and very handy indeed when you are trying to get your finances straight. It can also bring other welcome benefits, such as the opportunity to meet and make new friends. Many schemes run 'trade fairs', parties and other social events for members to get together and swap ideas and contacts. Supporting a scheme like this can be a very satisfying way of helping people in your community too.

OTHER SOURCES OF BARGAINS

There are many other methods and sources you can use to cut the price of goods and services. Here are a few of them:

- Look for shops that sell second-hand items. Remember, however, to check the condition of any items and ask if they come with any guarantees before purchasing.

- Go through the classified ads in newspapers and magazines to find items for sale at bargain prices.

- Try swapping items to get what you want. You could swap a colour television for a bicycle, for instance, or even exchange a car for a motor caravan. To find an online swap site, key the word 'swap' into any internet search engine, or check out the sites listed in Useful addresses (see pages 204–5).

Getting into good habits

I hope you have enjoyed looking at the many ways you can save money in this book. There's no need to stop here, though, because there are lots of other methods you can use to keep your costs down. Make it a habit to stay informed about new ways of cutting your expenses, and keep hunting for bargains. Don't just use these ideas

USEFUL ADDRESSES

The websites, clubs, companies and other organisations in this book are given for information purposes only and are not a recommendation. Always rely on your own research and check the credentials of organisations before you use their services.

Accountancy and legal services

THE INSTITUTE OF CHARTERED ACCOUNTANTS IN ENGLAND AND WALES
Chartered Accountants' Hall
PO Box 433
London EC2P 2BJ
Tel: 020 7920 8100
Fax: 020 7920 0547
Website: www.icaew.co.uk
Contact this organisation to find a chartered accountant in England or Wales.

THE INSTITUTE OF CHARTERED ACCOUNTANTS IN IRELAND
11 Donegall Square South
Belfast BT1 5JE
Tel: 02890 321600
Fax: 02890 230071
Website: www.icai.ie
Contact this organisation to find a chartered accountant in Ireland.

THE INSTITUTE OF CHARTERED ACCOUNTANTS OF SCOTLAND

CA House
21 Haymarket Yards
Edinburgh EH12 5BH
Tel: 0131 347 0100
Fax: 0131 347 0105
Website: www.icas.org.uk
This organisation will help you find a chartered accountant in Scotland.

THE LAW SOCIETY OF ENGLAND AND WALES

Ipsley Court
Berrington Close
Redditch
Worcs. B98 0TD
Tel: 0870 606 2500
Email: info.services@lawsociety.org.uk
Website: www.lawsociety.org.uk
Contact the Law Society to find a qualified solicitor in England or Wales.

THE LAW SOCIETY OF NORTHERN IRELAND

Law Society House
98 Victoria Street
Belfast BT1 3JZ
Tel: 02890 231614
Fax: 02890 232606
Email: info@lawsoc-ni.org
Website: www.lawsoc-ni.org
The Law Society of Northern Ireland will help you find a qualified solicitor in Northern Ireland.

THE LAW SOCIETY OF SCOTLAND

26 Drumsheugh Gardens

Edinburgh EH3 7YR

Tel: 0131 226 7411

Email: lawscot@lawscot.org.uk

Website: www.lawscot.org.uk

Contact the Law Society of Scotland to find a qualified solicitor in
Scotland.

Conservation organisations

ENGLISH HERITAGE

PO Box 569

Swindon SN2 2YP

Tel: 0870 333 1182

Email: customers@english-heritage.org.uk

Website: www.english-heritage.org.uk

The government's statutory adviser on the historic environment. It preserves
buildings and sites for the nation and gives privileges when you join.
Funding comes from the government, property revenues and memberships.

THE NATIONAL TRUST

PO Box 39

Warrington WA5 7WD

Tel: 0870 458 4000

Email: enquiries@thenationaltrust.org.uk

Website: www.nationaltrust.org.uk

This registered charity preserves over 300 historic houses, buildings and
gardens and 600 miles of coastline for the nation. Joining gives you free
entry and parking at their buildings and sites. You can also take working
holidays at a wide range of their UK sites.

Consumer protection and regulatory bodies

FINANCIAL SERVICES AUTHORITY

25 The North Colonnade

Canary Wharf

London E14 5HS

Consumer helpline: 020 7066 1000

Website: www.fsa.gov.uk

The FSA regulates the financial services industry and provides protection to savers and borrowers.

INFORMATION COMMISSIONER

Wycliffe House

Water Lane

Wilmslow

Cheshire SK9 5AF

Telephone helpline: 01625 545745

Fax: 01625 545510

Email: mail@ico.gsi.gov.uk

Website: www.informationcommissioner.gov.uk

As a consumer you have rights under the Data Protection Act regarding the way your personal data is used. If you are dissatisfied with the way a matter has been handled by a credit reference agency, or you have concerns about the way your personal information is being collected and used, you can contact the Information Commissioner and ask for assistance.

OFFICE OF FAIR TRADING

Fleetbank House

2–6 Salisbury Square

London EC4Y 8JX

Website: www.oft.gov.uk

If you are dissatisfied with the way a matter has been handled by a retailer or other business, you have certain rights as a consumer. You can write to the Office of Fair Trading and request assistance.

Credit reference agencies

CALLCREDIT PLC
PO Box 491
Leeds LS3 1WZ
Tel: 0870 060 1414
Website: www.callcredit.co.uk
Credit reference agency.

EQUIFAX PLC
Credit File Advice Centre
PO Box 1140
Bradford BD1 5US
Tel: 0870 010 0583
Website: www.equifax.co.uk
Credit reference agency.

EXPERIAN LIMITED
Consumer Help Service
PO Box 8000
Nottingham NG80 7WF
Tel: 0870 241 6212
Website: www.experian.co.uk
Credit reference agency.

Debt counsellors

BUSINESS DEBTLINE
Tricorn House
51–53 Hagley Road

Edgbaston
Birmingham B16 8TP
Tel: (freephone) 0800 197 6026
Website: www.bdl.org.uk
Provides guidance on many issues, from cash flows and making offers to creditors, to tax and insolvency. Callers receive a free information pack called 'Dealing with your Business Debts'.

CITIZENS ADVICE SCOTLAND
Spectrum House
2 Powderhall Road
Edinburgh EH7 4GB
Tel: 0131 550 1000
Website: www.cas.org.uk
The Scottish association is a separate body from the National Association of Citizens Advice Bureaux in England and Wales. It gives free advice to people in debt. Write or telephone to find a branch in your area, or log on to the website.

CONSUMER CREDIT COUNSELLING SERVICE (CCCS)
Wade House
Merrion Centre
Leeds LS2 8NG
Tel: (freephone) 0800 1381111
Email: contactus@cccs.co.uk
Website: www.cccs.co.uk
The CCCS is a charity with fully trained counsellors to help you sort out your personal finances free of charge.

NATIONAL ASSOCIATION OF CITIZENS ADVICE BUREAUX (NACAB)
Central Office
Myddelton House
115–123 Pentonville Road

London N1 9LZ

Tel: 020 7833 2181

Advice website: www.adviceguide.org.uk

The biggest single provider of free, confidential and independent debt advice in the UK. It delivers advice from over 2,000 different outlets across England and Wales. Write or telephone to find a branch in your area, or log on to the website. For Scotland, see Citizens Advice Scotland. For Northern Ireland, see Northern Ireland Association of Citizens Advice Bureaux.

NATIONAL DEBTLINE

Tricorn House

51–53 Hagley Road

Edgbaston

Birmingham B16 8TP

Tel: (freephone) 0808 808 4000

Website: www.nationaldebtline.co.uk

Runs a free national telephone helpline for people with debt problems in England, Wales and Scotland. It also produces a range of helpful factsheets, which it will send out free of charge to people in debt.

NORTHERN IRELAND ASSOCIATION OF CITIZENS ADVICE BUREAUX

11 Upper Crescent

Belfast BT7 1NT

Tel: 028 9023 1120

Website: www.citizensadvice.co.uk

The Northern Ireland association is a separate body from the National Association of Citizens Advice Bureaux in England and Wales. It gives free, confidential and independent advice to people in debt. Write or telephone to find a branch in your area, or log on to the website.

THE UK INSOLVENCY HELPLINE

Debt Advisory Service

National Administration Centre

788–790 Finchley Road

London NW11 7TJ

Tel: (freephone) 0800 074 6918

Website: www.insolvencyhelpline.co.uk

A national telephone helpline for people with debt problems in England, Wales, Scotland and Northern Ireland. The service is free, confidential and independent and is fully funded by the credit and insolvency industry.

WALES/CYMRU NATIONAL ASSOCIATION OF CITIZENS ADVICE BUREAUX

Unit 7

St Asaph Business Park

Glascoed Road

Llanelwy LL17 0LJ

Tel: 01745 586400

Website: www.adviceguide.org.uk

The Welsh association comes under the National Association of Citizens Advice Bureaux (NACAB) for England and Wales. It gives free, confidential and independent debt advice. To find a branch in your neighbourhood, you can telephone, write or log on to the website.

Entertainment for free

BBC TV

BBC Studio Audiences

PO Box 3000

BBC TV Centre

London W12 7RJ

Tel: 020 8576 1227

Website: www.bbc.co.uk

Offers free tickets for a wide range of television shows.

BELFAST TOURIST INFORMATION CENTRE

Belfast Welcome Centre
47 Donegall Place
Belfast BT1 5AD
Tel: 028 9024 6609
Website: www.gotobelfast.com
Information on free events and attractions going on in Belfast and the surrounding areas.

BIRMINGHAM TOURIST INFORMATION CENTRE

The Rotunda, 150 New Street
Birmingham B2 4PA
Tel: 0121 202 5099
Website: www.beinbirmingham.co.uk
Details of free attractions and events in and around Birmingham.

BRITISH WATERWAYS CANAL INFORMATION CENTRE

Cambrian House
Cambrian Wharf (off King Edwards Road)
Birmingham B78 3QZ
Tel: 0121 200 7400
Information on the canals and towpath walks in and around Birmingham.

CARDIFF TOURIST INFORMATION CENTRE

Cardiff Visitor Centre
16 Wood Street
Cardiff CF10 1ER
Tel: 029 2022 7281
Email: visitor@thecardiffinitiative.co.uk
Website: www.visitcardiff.info
Information on free events and attractions in Cardiff and the surrounding areas.

GLAMORGAN WALKS

Website: www.glamorganwalks.com

Details of hundreds of organised walks in and around the Cardiff area.

GLASGOW TOURIST INFORMATION CENTRE

Glasgow City Marketing Bureau

11 George Square

Glasgow G2 1DY

Tel: 0141 566 0800

Website: www.seeglasgow.com

A mine of information on free events and attractions in Glasgow and the
surrounding areas.

HARDEN'S LIMITED

14 Buckingham Street

London WC2N 6DF

Tel: 020 7839 4763

Email: info@hardens.com

Website: www.hardens.com

Publishes the invaluable guide called *London For Free*, which is packed
with information on free attractions in London.

ITV

Website: www.itv.com

Offers free tickets for a large number of television shows, such as *Who
Wants To Be A Millionaire?*, *Parkinson* and *It'll Be Alright on the Night*, in
London and in regional television centres around the country.

MANCHESTER TOURIST INFORMATION CENTRE

Town Hall Extension

Lloyd Street

St Peter's Square

Manchester M60 2LA

Tel: 0161 234 3157

Email: manchester.visitor.centre@manchester.gov.uk

Website: www.manchester.gov.uk/visitorcentre

All the information you need on free events and attractions in Manchester and the surrounding areas.

PLYMOUTH TOURIST INFORMATION CENTRE

Tourism Service

Plymouth City Council

Civic Centre

Plymouth PL1 2EW

Tel: 01752 266030 or 01752 306330

Email: marketing@plymouth.gov.uk

Website: www.visitplymouth.co.uk

All the information you need on free events and attractions in Plymouth and the surrounding areas.

Holiday bargains

THE CAMPING AND CARAVANNING CLUB

Greenfields House

Westwood Way

Coventry CV4 8JH

Tel: 02476 694995

Website: www.campingandcaravanningclub.co.uk

Runs campsites in the UK and helps organise camping trips abroad. Helps with cheaper travel and offers other useful discounts to help recoup your membership fee and keep holiday costs down.

CAMPING AND CARAVANNING UK

Website: camping.uk-directory.com

Has a directory that features 1,500 campsites around the UK. You can select sites near a beach, for example, or sites that allow dogs or have indoor swimming pools. Also has a guide to help you choose camping equipment, and a forum where knowledgeable people can help you with camping-related questions.

CHEAPEST CAMPING HOLIDAYS
Website: www.cheapest-camping-holidays.co.uk
Allows you to compare deals between a huge range of campsites in the UK and Europe, and deals on static and touring caravans.

DEE COOPER
Tel: 01764 670001 or 01764 679765
Website: www.livein-jobs.co.uk
Offers information on UK working holidays, such as hotel and bar jobs that pay a weekly wage and give free accommodation and food.

GTI HOME EXCHANGE
94 Fore Street
Bodmin
Cornwall PL31 2HR
Website: www.gti-home-exchange.com
If you would like to get free holiday accommodation by swapping homes with other people, you can register with this agency for a small fee and get access to a full list of their home-exchange members around the world.

HOMELINK INTERNATIONAL
7 St Nicholas Rise
Headbourne Worthy
Winchester
Hants. SO23 7SY
Tel: 01962 886882
Website: www.homelink.org.uk
Membership of this home-exchange agency gives you access to a full list of their members around the world.

LASTMINUTE.COM

Website: www.lastminute.com

Offers cut-price last-minute deals to a wide range of holiday destinations. An ideal way to cut your travel and accommodation costs.

PAYAWAY

Website: www.payaway.co.uk

Offers information and advice on a wide range of working holidays abroad, from skiing jobs in the Alps or camp-leader work in the United States to jobs in tourism, catering and teaching.

Property price checks

NETHOUSEPRICES

Website: www.nethouseprices.com

A free public service and promises that it always will be. Provides access to UK property prices in England, Scotland and Wales, as recorded by the Land Registry (since April 2000) and the Registers of Scotland (since May 2000).

Shopping for free and bargain hunting

BOOKER CASH & CARRY

Head Office

Equity House

Irthlingborough Road

Wellingborough

Northants. NN8 1LT

Tel: 01933 371000

Website: www.booker.co.uk

Has 177 branches around the UK, selling a wide range of cut-price products for businesses.

CAMLETS (LOCAL EXCHANGE AND TRADING SYSTEM)
Website: www.camlets.org
The website for Cambridge LETS, an alternative money system in Cambridge. It is a sophisticated barter system that allows local people to buy and provide services in the local alternative currency, called 'cams'. The site also provides links to LETS websites in other areas.

CATALOGUE BARGAIN SHOPS
Bargain Crazy Limited
Floor 2a Universal House
Devonshire Street
Ardwick
Manchester M60 6EL
Tel: 0161 277 1151 (helpdesk)
Website: www.bargaincrazy.com
Catalogue Bargain Shops have 30 branches around the country. You will find lots of ex-catalogue surplus goods here, from clothing and shoes to toys, household products and electrical goods. Anything, in fact, that you can find in the large mail-order catalogues. Discounts vary, so check prices against catalogue items and also against high-street prices to make sure you are getting a bargain.

CHESHIRE OAKS DESIGNER OUTLET
Junction 10, M53 motorway
Ellesmere Port
CH65 9JJ
Tel: 0151 348 5600
Website: www.mcarthurglen.com
You will find at least 30 per cent off top designer labels, and often more. There are 140 shops, which are open seven days a week, and parking is free.

EBAY

Website: www.ebay.co.uk

A well-established auction website, with over 135 million registered users worldwide. On the UK site alone, an item sells every half a second. You can buy and sell anything here, from antiques to travel tickets. The site does not make a charge to purchasers (apart from whatever price you have bid for the item), but sellers do have to pay a small fee.

EBID

Website: www.ebid.co.uk

This popular auction website is free to join and does not charge you for listing items you wish to sell. You pay a small fee only when you actually sell an item. You can buy and sell anything online, from antiques and jewellery to travel tickets and office goods.

THE FACTORY SHOP

Millennium Business Park

Station Road

Steeton

Keighley

West Yorkshire BD20 6RB

Tel: 01535 650950

Website: www.thefactoryshopltd.co.uk

Has at least 63 factory shops around England, Scotland, Wales and Northern Ireland, which sell a wide range of bargain products, including branded fashion clothing and footwear, household products, furniture, toys, giftware, lighting books, and soft furnishings. Many items are sold at 50 per cent off recommended retail prices.

FASHION-ERA

Website: www.fashion-era.com/factory_outlets_shopping.htm

Offers valuable information and advice about shopping for clothing. Also provides links to outlet shops and villages, and factory shops.

GENERAL AUCTIONS LIMITED

63–65 Garratt Lane

London SW18 4AA

Tel: 020 8870 3909

Fax: 020 8877 3583

Website: www.generalauctions.co.uk

Many bargains regularly fall under the hammer at these auctions, such as cheap bicycles and other goods, and stock from HM Revenue & Customs and various County Courts.

INTHEREFIRST

Website: www.intherefirst.com

Allows you to swap anything, from books and sports equipment to computer games and mobile phones. Also allows you to do trade-offs, whereby you offer an item or service in exchange for a different item or service. For example, if you need a plumber, you could offer to do some decorating in return, or offer an item you no longer need. If the value of an item or skill doesn't match its counterpart, you can even top it up with cash. There is also the facility to haggle for items. This is a wonderfully flexible way of bartering and exchanging goods and services. At the time of writing, all services on this site are free, but the site says this is for a limited period only, so make sure you check for any fees before going ahead.

KELKOO

Website: www.kelkoo.co.uk

This website lets you compare prices on a wide range of goods, from books, clothing and household appliances to sports, fitness equipment, travel and flights.

LETSLINK UK

Website: www.letslinkuk.org

There are over 450 independent LETS (Local Exchange and Trading Systems) in Britain that allow people to barter services, and these involve over 40,000 people. This website provides links to these schemes around the country, enabling you to locate the one nearest to you.

MAKRO SELF SERVICE WHOLESALERS LIMITED

Head Office

Liverpool Road

Barton Moss

Eccles

Manchester M30 7RT

Tel: 0870 16 62576

Website: www.makro.co.uk

Has 33 branches dotted around the UK, selling a wide range of cut-price foods and non-food products to business traders. It is part of Metro Group, which has trading outlets in 24 different countries.

SIMMONS J.C. & CO

Saltburn Salerooms

Diamond Street

Saltburn-by-Sea

Cleveland TS12 1EB

Tel: 01287 622366

Website: www.saltburnsalerooms.com

You can purchase a wide range of items at bargain prices here, including cheap bicycles and other modern consumer goods, and a wide variety of collectables and antiques.

SWAPZ.CO.UK

Website: www.swapz.co.uk

This website is free to join and allows you to swap anything you like, from DVDs and toys to household goods and cars. You can swap with other members of the site in the UK and worldwide.

TROLLYDOLLY

Website: www.trollydolly.co.uk

This website allows you to compare prices on a wide range of groceries, and other items such as clothes, music and entertainment.

GLOSSARY

Balance transfer: transfer of debt from one lender to another, such as moving an outstanding balance from one credit card to another.

Bankruptcy: once a person is declared bankrupt, all of his or her affairs are handed over to a Receiver, who will deal with them on the debtor's behalf and divide any monies raised from the sale of any assets between the creditors. During the term of the bankruptcy – now a minimum of one year – the debtor will not be able to borrow any money and will have to declare all income received. At the end of the term, all his or her debts will be cleared.

Compounding: in relation to interest, compounding means 'interest on the interest'. Basically, interest is added to the basic amount of a loan or investment at the end of a given period to form a new total figure for the next period. Further interest is then given on the original amount plus the interest to date.

Credit file: this file is kept by credit reference agencies and contains your personal financial information, including your current and past loans, and any unpaid debts or court actions. Information is stored on your file for six years.

Creditor: any person or organisation who is owed money.

Credit reference agency: an organisation that holds and maintains your credit file. At the time of writing there are three agencies: Experian, Equifax and Callcredit plc.

Credit scoring: a system for calculating a person's creditworthiness by adding up points awarded according to an individual's personal details, for example age, marital status, occupation and address.

Debit card: this is not a credit card. When you use a debit card, the money will be taken out of your bank account immediately. The transaction will not be permitted if there is insufficient money in your account at that time.

Debtor: a person who owes money.

Early redemption penalty: this is a charge levied by some lenders to compensate them for loss of interest in the event that the borrower pays off part or all of a loan quicker than originally agreed. Not all loans attract these penalties, but some do, so the borrower should check before proceeding.

Equity: the surplus value in your home after what you owe has been deducted.

Financial Services Authority (FSA): a powerful statutory regulator that provides valuable protection to the consumer. Its powers are wide-ranging and it can impose penalties for various offences, bring disciplinary proceedings and court actions, and can require compensation for consumers.

Fixed rate: if the interest rate on a loan is fixed, it will stay at the same rate for the period of time agreed, so you know in advance how much it will cost.

Interest: when you borrow money, interest is the lender's fee for loaning it to you; when you invest money, interest is the fee paid to you for letting someone else have the use of your money.

Introductory rate: a discounted rate of interest used to tempt new customers to join. For example, introductory rates on new credit cards can be as low as 0 per cent for an initial period, usually six months.

IVA (Individual Voluntary Agreement): an arrangement (England, Wales and Northern Ireland only) whereby you pay your debts from your surplus money after living expenses have been deducted. After five years, all debts, and interest, will be cleared. To qualify for an IVA, creditors who are owed a minimum of three-quarters of your overall debt must agree to it.

Money-back card: a credit card that pays you a percentage back of every purchase you make using the card. Also known as a cashback card.

Notice of Disassociation: if you wish to show to potential lenders that you are not financially connected to someone (for example, someone who has a bad debt and lives at your address), you can apply for a Notice of Disassociation to be placed on your credit file.

Personal financial statement (see Statement of means).

Replacement technique: method of replacing a costly item with a cheaper or free equivalent.

Secured loan: a loan secured against a valuable asset, which the lender can repossess if the loan repayments are not met.

Statement of means: a chart showing a person's financial situation, including full information about expenditure and income.

Switch card: this works in the same way as a debit card (see Debit card).

Trust Deed: a similar arrangement to the IVA but for Scottish residents only. You need to get only those creditors who are owed a minimum of two-thirds of your overall debt to agree to this, and at the end of three years all your debts and interest are cleared, but a person will be appointed to administer your affairs and you will have less control over your day-to-day finances.

Unsecured loan: a loan that has not been secured against a valuable asset, which means that if the borrower defaults, the lender has no automatic right to repossess an asset of value.

Variable rate: if the interest rate on a loan is variable, it can go up or down depending on market conditions, so you may end up paying more or less interest than you originally anticipated.

Working tax credit: this tax allowance is administered by HM Revenue & Customs. If you are a working person on a low income, you may be able to get it.

FURTHER READING

Clearing clutter and feng shui

Karen Kingston, *Clear Your Clutter with Feng Shui*, Piatkus, 1988
Karen Kingston, *Creating Sacred Space with Feng Shui*, Piatkus, 1996

Free entertainment and leisure

London For Free, Harden's Limited, 2003

Personal finance

Alvin Hall, *Money for Life*, Hodder & Stoughton, 2000
Alvin Hall, *Your Money or Your Life*, Hodder & Stoughton, 2002
Robert T. Kiyosaki, *Rich Dad, Poor Dad*, Warner Books, 2000
Robert T. Kiyosaki, *Rich Dad, Poor Dad 2: The Cashflow Quadrant*, Time Warner Paperbacks, 2002
Martin Lewis, *The Money Diet*, Vermilion, 2005

INDEX

Page numbers in *italic* are glossary entries.

A

accommodation cost savings 60–1

accountants 43, 167–8

Administration Order 31–2

advertising, encouragement to spend xiv–xv, 83–4

airlines, discounts 180–1

allowances *see* state benefits and allowances; tax allowances

alternative money schemes 185–6

auctions (buying at) 183–4

B

balance transfers 156–7, *207*

bank base rate 161

bank lending system 145–6

bankruptcy 24, 31–3, 34, 37, *207*

Bankruptcy Restriction Order (BRO) 33

barter schemes 185–6

benefits *see* state benefits and allowances

bereavement, checking insurance policies 44

bicycle, purchasing 67–8

bills
 budgeting for the unexpected 78–80
 ignoring 2
 starting to deal with 2–3

birthdays, spending on 6

borrowing *see* credit cards; loans; mortgages; personal loans

broadband, comparing charges 66

building society savings, interest rates 147–50

Business Debtline 26–7

C

Callcredit plc 34–5

camping holidays 177–80

car boot sales 51–2

car loans 141, 144–5

carer's allowance 41, 45

cash-and-carry shops 183

catalogue surplus shops 183

Christmas spending 6

Citizens Advice Bureau (CAB) xiv, xv, 23–4

classified ads 186

clutter
 converting to cash 46–53
 time wasted by 129

community care grant 41

compounding of interest 148, *207*

consolidation loans 19–20, 143

Consumer Credit Counselling Service (CCCS) 21–2, 83, 86–7

consumer debt problems, UK xiv–xv

correspondence, dealing with 129

court appearance, help with 24

credit cards 155–9, *207*, *209*

credit file 33–7, *207*

credit reference agencies 33–7, *207*

credit scoring *208*

creditors *207* see also debts

cycling 67–8

D

debit cards 158, *208*

debt problems in the UK xiv–xv

debtor *208*

debts

arranging to pay off 13–17

asking for interest to be frozen 15, 17

borrowing to cover 142–5

changes in finance companies 17

dealing with a monthly shortfall 10–11

dividing money between creditors 13–17

high cost of xv

moving to a cheaper lender 66

order of urgency 12–13

prioritising by interest rate 14

reasons for 1–2

writing to creditors 14–17

see also help sources

digital TV, comparing charges 66

E

e-mails, time spent on 130

eating out on a budget 89, 90–1

eBay 52–3

endowment policies 160–1

English Heritage 92

Equifax 34–5

equity *208*

Experian 34–5

F

factory shops 182–3

family

borrowing from 27–8

lending to 145, 146

fashion, encouragement to spend xv

financial advisers 150–2, 159, 163–4, 165, 167

financial assessment, from financial statement 11

financial health checks 168–9

financial services, making savings 66

Financial Services Authority (FSA) 150–1, *208*

financial shortfall, dealing with 10–11

financial statement (chart) 3–11, *209*

surplus/shortfall calculation 10–11

food bills, savings 68–70

free outings see outings and attractions for free

free professional help 20–7,
37
friends
always paying for 84–6
borrowing from 27–8
lending to 145, 146

G
gas and electricity savings
61–2

H
help sources
Business Debtline 26–7
Citizens Advice Bureau
(CAB) xiv, xv, 23–4
consolidation loans 19–20
143
Consumer Credit
Counselling Service
(CCCS) 21–2, 83, 86–7
for small businesses 24,
26–7
Money Advice Centres
25–6
National Debtline 22–3
plan for immediate action
11–17
professional help (free)
20–7, 37
professional help (with
fees) 19–20
HM Customs and Excise 27
HM Revenue and Customs
27, 42
holiday loans 142, 144–5
holiday spending 6
holidays on a budget or free
172–81
home
borrowing to purchase
141, 144–5
market value 28–30, *208*

repossession 28–31
home exchange holidays
173–4
hotels, discounts 180
house-sitting holidays 176–7
household expenses, sharing
45

I
impulse buying 2
income and outgoings chart
see financial statement
income
from insurance policies
43–4
increasing your earnings
44–5
listing 9–10
selling unwanted
possessions 46–53
state benefits and
allowances 40–1
tax credits 42
tax rebates 42
ways to increase 39, 45–6
Individual Voluntary
Arrangement *see* IVA
Inland Revenue 27
insurance
death-in-service policies 44
income from policies 43–4
mortgage repayments 163
payment protection policies
44
redundancy protection 43
savings on policy costs 64–6
interest 133–8, *208*
effect of loan time period
136–8
fixed and variable rates
136, *208*, *209*
on savings and investments
147–50

rate percentages 134–6
internet buying and selling
52–3, 183–4
introductory rates 156–7, *209*
investment, borrowing for
139–40, 144–5
IVA (Individual Voluntary
Arrangement) 24, 31–2,
209

J
joint finances 9, 82, 86

L
leisure activities on a
budget/free 89, 91–113
lending
bank lending system
145–6
good lending practice
145–6
investment interest 147–50
to friends and relatives
145, 146
to organisations 147–50
letter to creditor (sample) 16
letting a spare room 45–6
Lewis, Martin 70–1
loans (borrowing)
checking your interest rates
152
consolidation loans 19–20,
143
early redemption penalties
139, 161–2, *208*
fixed and variable interest
rates 136, *208*
from friends and family
27–8
getting the best deals
152
interest rates 133–8, *208*,
210

percentages 134–6
reasons for borrowing
139–45
secured and unsecured
30–1, 139–40, *209*
Social Fund 41
things you should find out
139–40
tie-ins 139
time period to pay back
136–8
to cover debts and
expenses 142–5
see also credit cards;
mortgages; personal
loans
local exchange and trading
systems (LETS) 185–6

M
mobile phone savings 64
Money Advice Centres 25–6
money-back cards 158–9,
209
money diary 73–81
money-making opportunities
see income
mortgages 159–64
capped rate 162
checking your interest rate
162
comparison websites
162–3
early redemption penalties
161–2, *208*
endowment policies 160–1
fixed rate of interest
161–2, *208*
getting help with payments
40
interest-only 159, 160–1
mortgage cost savings
60–1

mortgage repayment
insurance 163
repayment 159–60
security 163
standard variable rate of
interest 161, 162, *210*
switching 163–4
tie-in periods 161–2, 163
ways of charging interest
161–2, *208*, *210*
motoring costs 66–7
multitasking 130, 131

N
National Debtline 22–3
National Trust 91–2, 176
nights out on a budget 89,
90–1

O
outgoings
listing 3, 5–9
making savings 59–71
replacement technique
56–9, *209*
unexpected bills 78–80
unnecessary spending
55–6
see also spending
outings and attractions for
free 89, 91–113
around the UK 112–13
Belfast 108–12
Birmingham 96–9
Cardiff 102–4
Glasgow 104–8
London 93–5
Manchester 100–2
Plymouth 95–6
outlet shops and villages
182–3
overspending *see* spending
habits

overwork and stress 126–8

P
partner *see* joint finances
payment protection policies
44
percentages 134–6
personal loans 164–5
petrol costs 67
professional help (free) 20–7,
37
professional help (with fees)
19–20
property investment,
borrowing for 139–40,
144–5
Protected Trust Deed
(Scotland) 31–2, *210*

R
Receiver 32–3
redundancy payments 43–4
remortgaging, investment
property 140
replacement technique 56–9,
209
repossession 28–31

S
sales 181
savings and investments
147–52, 166–7
season tickets for travel 67
second-hand shops 186
secured and unsecured loans
139–40, *209*
selling over the Internet 52–3
selling unwanted possessions
46–53
shopping, cutting costs 181–6
small businesses 24, 26–7,
42–3
Social Fund loan 41

socialising on a budget 89, 90–1
spending
  advice and counselling 82–3
  compulsive spending 82–3
  impulse buying 2
  money diary 73–81
  overspending on other people 84–7
  reasons for overspending 82–4
  ways to control 82–7
  see also outgoings
spending money (day-to-day expenses) 7
state benefits and allowances 40–1, 45
stress and overload 126–8
student debt 1
student loans 1, 33
swapping 186
Switch cards 158, *209*

T
tax advisers 167–8
tax allowances and credits 42–3
tax liability, reducing 167–8
tax rebates 42
tax relief 42–3
telephone
  bill savings 62–4
  time spent on 129
television, time spent on 130
tenancy agreements 45–6
time
  managing effectively 125–31
  planning 118–25
  value of 115–18
travel costs, savings 66–8, 179, 180–1

Trust Deed 31–2, *209*

U
UK Insolvency Helpline 24

W
water bill savings 62
websites
  auctions 67–8, 183–4
  broadband charges comparison 66
  camping holidays 179–80
  catalogue surplus shops 183
  daily newspapers 57
  digital TV charges comparison 66
  eBay 53
  factory and outlet shops 182–3
  food price comparisons 70
  HM Revenue and Customs 42
  home exchanges 174
  house-sitting agencies 177
  insurance quotations 65
  Internet selling 52–3
  local exchange and trading systems (LETS) 185–6
  Martin Lewis 70–1
  mobile phone tariffs 64
  money-saving expert 70–1
  mortgage calculators 60–1
  mortgage comparisons 162–3
  state benefits 42
  stock market information 57
  swap sites 186
  tax credits 42
  telephone bill savings 63–4
  water bill savings 62
  weather forecasts 51

working holidays 174,
175–6
wholesalers 183
working holidays 174–6
working tax credit 210

Y
young workers, debt
problems 1–2

The Money Diet
Martin Lewis

Want to save thousands of pounds?
Just follow this simple money diet.

The average person spends more money on their telephone bill than stocks and shares, so why do finance books always talk about the markets? Whether it's utilities, credit cards, DVDs or debt, this fully updated edition of the bestselling *The Money Diet* holds the secret of how to get more money in your pocket. Martin Lewis could save you up to £6,000 a year with his easy to implement, cutting-edge advice.

HOW TO WIN FRIENDS AND INFLUENCE PEOPLE

Over 16 million copies sold

DALE CARNEGIE

THIS BOOK HAS THE POTENTIAL TO CHANGE YOUR LIFE

How to Win Friends and Influence People

Dale Carnegie

The most famous confidence-boosting book ever published

Dale Carnegie offers solid, practical advice that has stood the test of time and will help you get out of a mental rut and make your life more rewarding. You'll learn how to make friends quickly and easily, win people over to your way of thinking and become a more entertaining conversationalist. *How to Win Friends and Influence People* has the potential to change your life.

Also available from Vermilion

☐ The Money Diet   9780091906887   £7.99
☐ Your Idea Can Make
     You Rich   9780091909154   £12.99
☐ How to Win Friends and
     Influence People   9780091906818   £7.99
☐ Who Moved My Cheese? 9780091912734   £5.99

FREE POSTAGE AND PACKING
Overseas customers allow £2.00 per paperback

BY PHONE: 01624 677237

BY POST: Random House Books
C/o Bookpost, PO Box 29, Douglas
Isle of Man, IM99 1BQ

BY FAX: 01624 670923

BY EMAIL: bookshop@enterprise.net

Checques (payable to Bookpost) and credit cards accepted

Prices and availability subject to change without notice.

Allow 28 days for delivery.

When placing your order, please mention if you do not wish to receive
any additional information.

www.randomhouse.co.uk